PENGUIN
SELF-
STARTERS

Personnel Management

Denis Preston was born in 1917. His education at Cambridge and County High School and Acton Technical College was interrupted by ill-health but he gained senior managerial experience in hospital work, the chemical industry and engineering construction before entering further education at Garnett College in 1951. After pioneering developments in Management Studies for industry and the public services, he retired from senior college management in 1982.

He now occupies himself writing, lecturing to police officers and engaging in community projects; he is a Reader in the dioceses of Birmingham and Bangor. Married to a former senior youth organizer, he has two children.

SERIES EDITORS: Stephen Coote and Bryan Loughrey

Personnel Management

Denis Preston

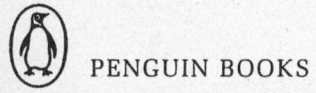
PENGUIN BOOKS

For Olive, Nicholas and Sarah

PENGUIN BOOKS

Published by the Penguin Group
27 Wrights Lane, London W8 5TZ, England
Viking Penguin Inc., 40 West 23rd Street, New York, New York 10010, USA
Penguin Books Australia Ltd, Ringwood, Victoria, Australia
Penguin Books Canada Ltd, 2801 John Street, Markham, Ontario, Canada L3R 1B4
Penguin Books (NZ) Ltd, 182–190 Wairau Road, Auckland 10, New Zealand

Penguin Books Ltd, Registered Offices: Harmondsworth, Middlesex, England

First published 1989
10 9 8 7 6 5 4 3 2 1

Copyright © Denis Preston, 1989
All rights reserved

Filmset in Linotron 202 Melior

Typeset, printed and bound in Great Britain by
Hazell Watson & Viney Limited
Member of BPCC plc
Aylesbury, Bucks, England

Except in the United States of America, this book is sold subject to
the condition that it shall not, by way of trade or otherwise, be lent,
re-sold, hired out, or otherwise circulated without the publisher's
prior consent in any form of binding or cover other than that in which
it is published and without a similar condition including this
condition being imposed on the subsequent purchaser

Contents

Acknowledgements	7
How to use this book	9
Introduction	11

The Case Studies

1	Carbits Ltd	15
2	Process Engineering PLC	26
3	Far Travel Ltd	35
4	Heavy Engineering Ltd	40
5	Scraps & Scrap Ltd	43
6	Auto Processing Ltd	46
7	Goldwares Ltd	49
8	The International	54
9	Chemcon PLC	59
10	Wiring Work PLC	65
11	Automobiles PLC	70
12	Weatherwear Ltd	76
13	ReproSelect Ltd	81
14	Fabricators and Finishers Ltd	85
15	Econclothiers Ltd	89
16	The Component Co. Ltd	92
17	Finishing Productions PLC	96
18	Anticorro PLC	101
19	L & L Ltd	108
20	Buns & Buns Ltd	111
21	Fine Enamels PLC	114
22	The Brass Man Ltd	119
23	Shoddy & Co. Ltd	122
24	Finery Ltd	125
25	Switchon PLC	129
26	Electro Gadgets PLC	133
27	Boxes Ltd	137

Contents

28	Stones and Settings Ltd	140
29	Artistic Products Ltd	143
30	News & Food PLC	148
31	The Beach House Café	151

Appendices

I	Equal Opportunities Commision	154
II	Commission for Racial Equality	155
III	Advisory, Conciliation and Arbitration Service	156
IV	Department of Employment's regional offices	157
V	Some useful booklets	158

Acknowledgements

To attempt to list the names of all the many people to whom I am grateful would inevitably lead to accidental omissions; but I cannot fail to mention most particularly my debt to Mrs Doris Wheatley, without whose initial encouragement the book would not have been written; to Mrs Joan Maughan, a former secretary, who in her retirement tackled my handwriting once again and produced the typed drafts from which the final copies were made; to Mrs Lyn Middleton, who typed the final scripts; and to my wife, Olive, and my children, Nicholas and Sarah, for their patient encouragement.

Disclaimer

Although the situations described in the case studies below have all occurred in real life, none of the companies or individuals named in them are based on actual companies or individuals. If readers think they recognize themselves or companies known to them in these pages, the author assures them that they are mistaken and that all the situations specifically described have been drawn from his imagination.

How to use this book

This book may be used by individuals or by groups. It consists of an Introduction, which lays down certain ideas and principles, followed by a series of case studies in which situations are shown developing that require remedial action, either there and then or in order to avoid similar problems arising in the future.

Case studies as a method of learning are often used, because they enable the reader to perceive the great complexity of personality, motivation, management structure and 'politics', as well as legal requirements and constraints, that make up the typical 'management problem'. The case study is preferable to a straightforward exposition alone; while someone with a good memory and some instinct for the law can memorize rules, it does not follow that the same person can either circumvent problems or, if they occur, know how to solve them.

In most of the case studies described in this book the problem has already reached the point where it is extremely serious; this has been done so that the reader may see the complete pattern of events. It is to be hoped that through careful examination of the case studies readers will learn how to avoid similar disasters in their own organizations.

The individual temperament and needs of the reader will dictate the actual method of using this book. Each case study is complete in itself and is followed by a Reference Section. Each case can be studied in one of two ways:

1. The case study can be read and then discussed, its problems analysed and possible responses considered, after which the Reference Section page can be read and further discussion and study undertaken.
2. The case study and Reference Section can be read without any interlude for consideration and possible discussion.

How to use this book

As you read the case studies you will notice that they contain a great amount of detail. This is because real life is full of detail and dealing with management problems involves taking into account much information that at first appears trivial but is really necessary to a proper understanding of the difficulty and its correct solution. Because of this, you will probably find that each case study will lead you to consider organizational and ethical issues as well as legal requirements. This is as it should be, since the management of people involves much more than blindly following the letter of the law.

When reading organizational charts and diagrams, it is necessary to realize that they can give an indication of only the formal structure of a company; in practice, there is also an informal structure, which is not capable of being easily expressed in diagrammatic form. The informal structure comprises those powerful individuals whose personalities, long service or acknowledged expertise give them a degree of influence that may not be reflected by their position in the formal structure.

In addition to these employees, there is often another group of people – for example, secretaries and personal assistants – who can often exercise a subtle but very important influence by their ability to control and manipulate access to senior management, by their power to control the use of time by organizing diary entries, and by their place within the organization's system of communication. In each case study, you need to consider the possibility that there may be disharmony between the formal and informal structures.

In order to gain the fullest benefit from these case studies you will need to obtain copies of all the booklets referred to in Appendix V, pp. 158–9. They can usually be obtained from your local Jobcentre or from the area or regional offices of the appropriate government department. Unlike Acts of Parliament, these booklets are free. They will give you a good understanding of the major laws that affect people working in industry and commerce. They explain the law in an easily understood form, but, of course, in any hearing before a law court or tribunal, it is the actual Act of Parliament and regulations made under it that count.

Introduction

Management is about dealing with people and things. Things are comparatively easy to manage because they obey various known laws of science and can be counted and organized without our provoking any protest from them. People are different! They do not obey any known laws of behaviour and do not accept organization and arrangement without comment, possibly protests – or even refusal. Each person has all the rights, moral and legal, that our society accepts as fair and proper.

Because organization as it affects people is complicated by emotional, moral and legal issues, there has come into being a group of specially educated and trained people who have made a study of what is called 'personnel management'. These individuals, usually called 'personnel managers' or 'personnel officers', are not normally 'line managers'; that is, they are not responsible for the operational aspects of the business. They give advice on personnel issues and they organize, in conjunction with the 'line management', such matters as staff selection, dismissal, redundancy, training, welfare and industrial relations. They often have great influence on the day-to-day operation of the business and sometimes even on policy. This book is not really intended for such highly trained men and women, though they may find the case studies interesting; rather, it is for those people who manage small and medium-sized companies, which do not necessarily employ trained personnel managers.

If you are managing a business without having had any specific training in personnel matters, you are probably beginning to realize that you have to master at least the fundamentals of the industrial legislation dealing with people and to understand the purposes and powers of industrial tribunals, the Advisory, Conciliation and Arbitration Service (ACAS), the Equal Opportunities Commission and the Commission for Racial Equality. You can begin to do this by studying the booklets referred to and, when in doubt, by seeking the advice of the organizations just mentioned, as well as your local Health and Safety Executive and other government departments.

However, if you concentrate exclusively on matters of law, you will fail as a manager, for good managers are aware of other people – their characters, qualities, weaknesses and strengths, personal problems and ambitions – and maintain a continuous and caring relationship with all those in their area of control. This does not mean that you should tolerate poor standards of work or conduct, but it does mean that you should always be alert to the potential difficulties arising from interpersonal relations, including, of course, relations with you, the manager.

Sound management will demand from you honesty, candour, decisiveness and firmness coupled with sensitivity and tact; if you display the latter two qualities without the former ones, however, you will end up being weak and ineffectual. This does not mean that you should distort your own personality in an effort to make it correspond with some kind of management persona or image that is at variance with your true self. If you try to manage in that way, your staff will soon see through the falseness such a method produces.

All this should lead you to develop an attitude of wariness and caution whenever you have to make decisions affecting employees. Perhaps most of all you will need to cultivate a patient readiness (sometimes in the face of difficulties and provocation) to listen to explanations, even when the likelihood of these being of value seems remote. This quality of patience in the pursuit of justice and fairness is summed up in the following words of a distinguished lawyer, Sir Robert Megarry. You and every other manager need to read them, believe in their value and strive to practise what they recommend.

> It may be that there are some who would decry the importance which the courts attach to the observance of the rules of natural justice. 'When something is obvious,' they may say, 'why force everybody to go through the tiresome waste of time involved in framing charges and giving an opportunity to be heard? The result is obvious from the start.' Those who take this view do not, I think, do themselves justice. As everybody who has anything to do with the law well knows, the path of the law is strewn with examples of open and shut cases which, somehow, were not; of unanswerable charges which, in the event, were completely answered; of inexplicable conduct which was fully explained; of

fixed and unalterable determinations that, by discussion, suffered a change. Nor are those with any knowledge of human nature who pause to think for a moment likely to underestimate the feelings of resentment of those who find that a decision against them has been made without their being afforded any opportunity to influence the course of events.

The Case Studies

1 Carbits Ltd

'Why are they so touchy?'

This case study concerns problems at the firm of Carbits Ltd, whose general organization is indicated by the diagram on p. 16.

Carbits is a relatively straightforward organization and its formal and informal structures are in harmony. From the diagram it will be noticed that the only people possessing line management, or direct control, of branch managers are the General Manager and Chairwoman. The Company Secretary, the Sales Manager and the Buyer have no direct line of command in respect of branch managers, but their senior positions and their relationships with both the General Manager and the Chairwoman give them great influence. Inevitably their communications, especially those of the Company Secretary and the Sales Manager, are accepted in day-to-day practice by the branch managers as being instructions, partly because of the expertise of the writers and partly because they could claim to be acting on behalf of the General Manager.

Put yourself in the role of the General Manager of this very successful firm engaged in the retail distribution of motor spares and accessories. You are 42 years old and have held your present appointment for three years. Before that, you were sales manager, having risen from the position of branch manager. You are an experienced motor vehicle parts expert and are especially concerned with the profitable purchasing of parts and accessories.

The firm is a private limited company. The Chairwoman and

The Case Studies

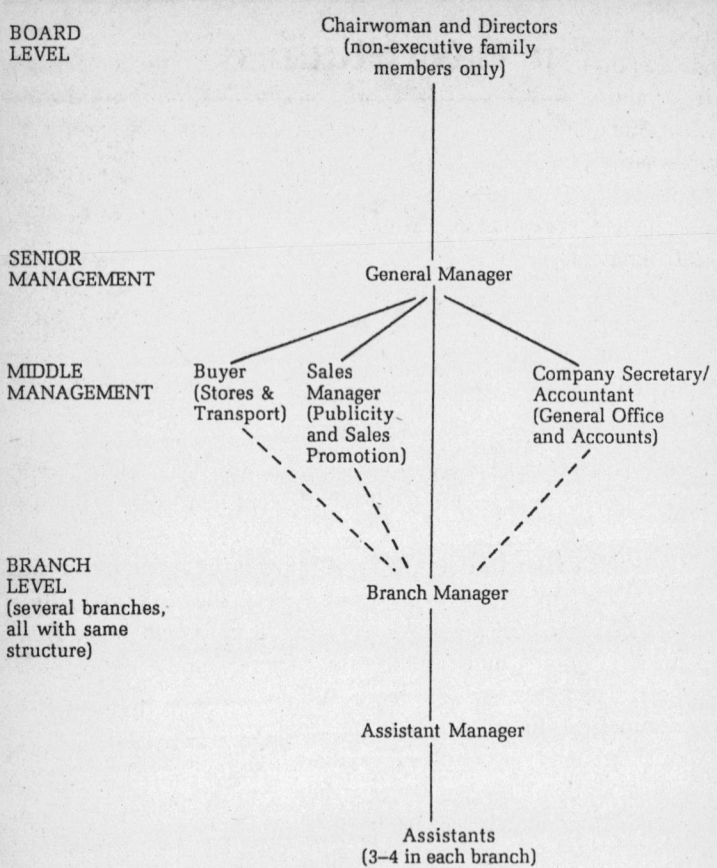

BOARD LEVEL — Chairwoman and Directors (non-executive family members only)

SENIOR MANAGEMENT — General Manager

MIDDLE MANAGEMENT — Buyer (Stores & Transport); Sales Manager (Publicity and Sales Promotion); Company Secretary/Accountant (General Office and Accounts)

BRANCH LEVEL (several branches, all with same structure) — Branch Manager

Assistant Manager

Assistants (3–4 in each branch)

Line management (involving direct authority) ——————

Staff roles (involving provision of expert knowledge and support to those engaged in line management) – – – – – – –

Carbits Ltd

principal shareholder is a former senior police officer, aged 52, who took over the business on the death of her father. She is an intelligent, kindly and straightforward woman, conservative in her style and with rather old-fashioned formality of manner. She has always loved motor cars and, though not a parts expert, has no difficulty in grasping the technical issues. Her police experience has made her familiar with the use of computers. Perhaps because of her background she has a liking for the presentation of a clear, well-researched, written report before she makes any final decision. 'Let's have the evidence,' as she says.

The company has seven branches, widely located in a densely populated industrial area covering about 300 square miles. Each branch consists of a well-appointed shop in a main shopping street, each shop being staffed by a branch manager, an assistant manager, several assistants and a cashier.

The company's staff policy has perhaps been affected by the experience of the Chairwoman, who prefers internal promotions whenever possible and prides herself on the personal and friendly relations that exist between herself and her staff. Occasionally this policy has been ignored, the last time being on the appointment of the Sales Manager. He is 35 and came from a similar company operating in Devon and Cornwall that has more branches, divided into areas. He held an appointment as area sales manager and had hoped to become sales manager, but was defeated by another area sales manager, an extremely spirited and energetic married woman of his own age.

The Company Secretary/Accountant of Carbits is another outside appointment. Now aged 60, he was appointed to the post on his retirement from the Royal Army Pay Corps by the present Chairwoman's father. He is a very competent financial controller and has been responsible for the computerization.

The situation with which you are now faced is this: one of the branch managers, who has charge of the firm's most prosperous branch, is about to retire, aged 65. He has always been a loyal, hard-working man – but, if the truth be told, the success of the branch stems more from its excellent location than from any great skill on his part. He has been fortunate in that his cashier is interested in the computer, and his assistant manager, though young, is noted for his technical skill and knowledge. (He was, in fact, promoted by you.) This young man is not applying for the job as manager, as he is currently working hard for an Open University degree.

The impending vacancy has been advertised internally and two of the existing managers and two of the assistant managers have applied. For an existing manager the main advantage is the possibility of earning more commission, since all branch managers are paid the same basic salary. For assistant managers there is a marked rise in basic salary as well as the kudos promotion brings.

Of the two managers who have applied, one has been rejected, ostensibly on the grounds that he is very close to retirement (he is 63), but in fact because he is not happy with the new computer system and would find himself under extreme pressure at a busy branch. The other three applicants have been interviewed jointly by the Sales Manager and the Company Secretary/Accountant; there is no personnel manager at Carbits, since the Chairwoman holds the view that personnel management in a medium-sized firm does not warrant a specialized appointment.

The Applicants

The persons interviewed were:

Winston He is 28, single, of West Indian origin and has had six years' service with the company, starting as an assistant; he is currently an assistant manager at a busy branch. He has four 'O'-level certificates, speaks well and is a young man of good appearance. He is very interested in motor cars and, after some initial problems in finding work, joined the parts department of a large distributor of Japanese vehicles, which also provided service facilities for other makes of car. After five years with that firm, he joined your company. He has an excellent understanding of the computerized stock system and is a man of very real ability. However, his self-confident temperament and rather impulsive enthusiasm, coupled with his comparative lack of experience, lead him at times to substitute a rather flighty charm for exact knowledge.

He is extremely hard-working and anxious to please and is improving steadily. Staff, unless racially prejudiced, get on well with him; since his appointment as assistant manager there has been only one difficult incident, when a van driver, a heavily tattooed skinhead, threatened him with violence following a row over who should unload the van. On that occasion Winston behaved with considerable calm and resolution and, in the absence of his branch manager and supported by his assistants and the motherly fury of the middle-aged cashier, persuaded the driver to do as he was told.

Marion She is 34 and is currently an assistant manager. She is divorced and has two children, aged 14 and 12. She is believed to be contemplating remarriage and in the past has frequently expressed the wish to have two more children.

She previously worked for many years in the domestic equipment department of a large retail store. She left this concern for domestic reasons and later took up an appointment with your company, mainly because of its convenient location when the children were younger. She has risen to her present position during the four years she has been with Carbits.

Marion has a remarkable memory and great ability as an organizer. She has a strong belief in order, thoroughness and discipline. Her grasp of the business has been acquired by practice and at present she has in fact only a modest understanding of the complicated aspects of the trade, although a genuine interest in motor cars and a determination to learn is causing her to expand her knowledge. Her customer relations are excellent, her communication skills are very good, and her style and appearance are impressive.

Staff either like or dislike her strongly: there seem to be no half measures. In the past there have been some angry scenes, from which she has always emerged victorious, the defeated person usually leaving soon afterwards. In these incidents Marion has always been supported by her manager, a mild man with mainly technical interests, who has been happy to rely upon her forceful methods. To staff who have accepted her style of management she is unswervingly loyal, supportive and kind-hearted.

She is a staunch feminist; she suffered much at the hands of her former husband, who could fairly be described as an extreme example of male chauvinism. Unlike most of the staff, Marion is a keen trade-unionist.

Patrick He is 50, married and has a grown-up family. He has been a manager for ten years, having joined Carbits from a rival organization that had run into financial difficulties, caused by mismanagement by its board. To avoid unemployment, he took an assistant's job but was promoted within eighteen months to the post of assistant manager and, after two more years, to his present position. As a youth, he was apprenticed as a motor vehicle mechanic and was engaged in service work for some years. His present branch is functioning successfully despite its rather unfavourable location – about half a mile away from a main branch of a national chain of motor spare parts shops.

Patrick rather despises modern computer technology, which is not entirely surpising since his long experience and formidable powers of visualization and memory have given him the ability to recall parts and their variations for model after model dating back many years. This, coupled with his practical knowledge, frequently enables him to react to customers' inquiries ahead of the computer stock-list and occasionally to suggest alternatives, which the computer cannot do. His manner with customers resembles that of a rather autocratic consultant surgeon making a diagnosis and proposing a course of treatment to a somewhat dull patient! Those who survive this always come back, so Patrick has built up a large group of satisfied and loyal customers, who recommend him enthusiastically to their friends.

With his staff the same style prevails. Young men are sometimes antagonized, young women rarely, if only because he is really a kindly man with an old-fashioned willingness to accept from women, especially from girls, what he would not from young men. His mother was a nursing sister and his father, whom he greatly admires, a regimental sergeant major in the Irish Guards – indeed only his poor eyesight and lack of height prevented Patrick from joining his father's regiment.

The Interviewing Panel's Reports

The candidates have been interviewed individually by the Sales Manager and the Company Secretary/Accountant. Their report and recommendations are as follows:

Carbits Ltd

Winston He is a neat and well-set-up young man of some potential, presently in the right job. He needs more experience and must take care over his attitude. For example, when asked about the incident with the van driver and questioned as to why, when threatened with violence, he had not summoned the police, he said that while the affair did not warrant police action he would in any event have expected them to take the side of the skinhead, who was white. It was pointed out to him that the branch at which the vacancy occurred lay in a district with few West Indian residents and that this would be a disadvantage to him; he appeared to resent the observation. Asked about his ambitions for the future, he stated that he had hopes of rising to a senior post but that he feared he would not succeed since some people had expressed the view that he had already advanced too far too rapidly. He declined to name these people but said that he doubted whether members of ethnic minorities had the same chances as others. He appears to have a chip on his shoulder. He has two convictions for speeding.

Marion She is a very able woman but lacks technical understanding and is too dependent on 'information systems'. When asked about her marital and domestic plans, she became very angry and expressed the view that this was her business and that the law demanded that she be given the same chances as a man. 'You are making motherhood a bar' was one of the things she said. In view of her trade union membership, she was asked if she would approve of an increase in such membership in the firm; she said she would encourage it. She is not really suitable for the current post but should perhaps be considered for appointment when possible to a post at headquarters.

Patrick Throughout his interview, he displayed his customary bluntness of manner. Asked what he would do if appointed, he replied that he promised to 'knock them into shape at the branch', adding, 'There's too much slackness about these days!' He is a man of great experience and seems to have done very well in a branch where local competition is severe. The assistant manager at the branch where there is the vacancy is a Sikh, but Patrick has never expressed any doubts concerning the ability of men of this culture;

some years ago, in fact, he was instrumental in obtaining promotion for a very clever assistant who happened to be a Ugandan Asian.

The following recommendations are made:

- Patrick to be appointed
- Marion to be transferred to HQ as soon as possible
- Winston to be left where he is
- The post vacated by Patrick to be advertised both internally and externally.

Your Task

Having read this report, you are required to advise your company's Chairwoman on the decisions to be made. In particular, you are required to give your views on the correct appointment, but you may also wish to:

- give your recommendations on whether there should be any changes in selection methods;
- make recommendations as to what needs to be said to Winston and Marion, and the correct planning of any future training and experience.

Reference section

In considering the situation caused by the vacancy and the subsequent interviews, you should take the following factors into account.

1. The appointment: either one of the internal candidates can be appointed or an exception to the rule can be made and the position advertised publicly.
2. The policy of favouring internal appointments has many advantages, provided previous staff selection has been effective in creating a body of staff from which promotions can be made and salaries and conditions of service are such as to make waiting for internal promotion attractive. The policy of internal promotions, when coupled with a

stable, slowly changing staff, should enable members of staff to foresee likely opportunities. Should a situation arise in which the majority of the staff, including the managers, are relatively young, it is likely that there will be steady losses among the lower levels of staff, to whom promotion will seem impossibly distant.

Internal promotions, while producing feelings of solidarity and loyalty, may also result in a very conservative attitude, with a distaste for innovation and a degree of complacency. Therefore it may well be best to maintain a policy by which internal candidates, all things being equal, are favoured, but inferior persons are not promoted simply because they are already on the staff. Lack of specialized expertise, enthusiasm or power to innovate must not be tolerated just to maintain the policy of internal promotions.

3. In making any recommendations to the Chairwoman, you need to consider urgently the dangers created by the apparent insensitivity of those conducting the interviews, both to the feelings of the candidates and to the legal implications. Doubts must have arisen in the minds of the candidates about the interviewers' freedom from serious prejudices in respect of sex, race and trade-union rights. You may have to give serious consideration to training management staff in personnel matters, particularly current legislation (see 5 below).

4. In drawing attention to the fact that these interviews may have endangered the firm, your recommendations to the Chairwoman may include the suggestion that the two candidates who are likely to have felt aggrieved be re-interviewed, their futures discussed and their fears of discrimination removed.

5. All this must point to the need to give serious thought to staff training. In your report to the Chairwoman you may wish to recommend as a matter of urgency a programme that will acquaint all those who are concerned with management (including junior management at branch level) with the law (see below). You may also voice the opinion

that those members of senior staff concerned with personnel selection be advised to review their methods of interviewing. In particular, you may like to consider whether:

- there should be a preliminary interview in which all the candidates meet the staff over whom the successful candidate will preside;
- all candidates should be asked the same basic questions, with supplementary questions arising spontaneously from their answers;
- different members of the interviewing panel could be assigned distinct and separate areas in which to put forward questions;
- the interviewing panel should be increased in size; for example, should not you and the Buyer have taken part?
- special training in interviewing, either within the company or at a further education centre, should be arranged for all managerial staff.

Before making your recommendations, you are advised to undertake further study of the following legislation:

- Sex Discrimination Act 1975
- Race Relations Act 1976
- Employment Acts 1980 and 1982.

Useful summaries of these Acts can be obtained from Jobcentres. In connection with this case study, you should look at:

- *Racial Discrimination: A Guide to the Race Relations Act 1976*, p. 8, paragraph 3.7; and *Sex Discrimination: A Guide to the Sex Discrimination Act 1975*, p. 8, paragraph 3.6, which state: 'It is unlawful for an employer to discriminate in the way he affords an employee access, or by refusing or deliberately omitting to afford access, to opportunities for promotion, transfer or training or to any other benefits, facilities or services. This covers the arrangements made for selection for promotion, transfer, or training, as well as the actual selection itself . . .'

- *Employment Acts 1980 and 1982*, p. 14. '. . . Employees are entitled to a remedy from an Industrial Tribunal if they have . . . action taken against them, as individuals, to prevent or deter them from belonging to a trade union or from taking part in union activities at an appropriate time – or as a penalty for so doing.'

In addition, you should read the *Code of Practice* of the Commission for Racial Equality; it gives very useful and specific guidance for training employees who have to select personnel for employment or promotion.

2 Process Engineering PLC

'Let's go for quality!'

Process Engineering PLC of Barnborough, West Yorkshire, is a very successful company engaged in the design and supply of plant and equipment for a variety of industries involved principally in continuous production processes. It has managed to avoid any unnecessary increases in its office and administrative staff and is considered to be one of the most economically run companies of its kind. It never takes on too many contracts and the quality of its design and site work is such that it maintains excellent relationships with old customers while steadily increasing the demand for its services.

Of late, however, it has had a serious loss from its ranks of HQ staff in the unexpected resignation (on a pension to which he is entitled) of one of its oldest and most devoted employees, a widower who has been persuaded by his only child to join him and his wife and children in California. This has caused a serious gap in the organization, since there is no member of the staff free to undertake the work he did as External Progress Officer.

To cope with the situation, for there is very little time to spare, the following advertisement has been placed in a trade journal, a quality national newspaper and the local daily paper.

> EXTERNAL PROGRESS OFFICER
> Process Engineering PLC requires a person to ensure the delivery, in accordance with construction plans, of plant and equipment being erected at sites throughout the United Kingdom.
>
> The successful candidate will have excellent powers of communication, strong negotiating skills with suppliers' staff at all levels, and the ability to maintain continuous

and effective liaison with the design, buying and construction staff of this company.

Although professional engineering qualifications are not essential, the successful candidate will possess the ability rapidly to grasp the essentials of technical problems and be able to offer constructive suggestions to the staff concerned, including suppliers.

The duties of the post may involve travelling to suppliers and to site and sometimes require long hours of work. Clerical support will be provided.

There is no upper age limit but the minimum age for candidates is 25 years.

The post is pensioned and the present salary range is between £10,500 and £13,500. A company car will be provided and there are various fringe benefits.

This company is an equal opportunities employer. Applications should be made at once with full details and the name of two referees to the Company Secretary, Process Engineering PLC, Barnborough, West Yorks BB2 5QL.

The Interviewers

The appointing panel consists of:

Nigel: the company's Buyer. Nigel is 58, an extremely practical, experienced man who has risen steadily, as the company has expanded, from junior clerk to his present appointment. His academic education was modest and he has no formal purchasing qualifications. However, his knowledge of the practice of purchasing is formidable, while his understanding of sources of supply and the goods and materials required is extremely wide ranging and up to date. He lives for three things: his work, his family and the breeding of pedigree tabby cats; indeed, he has grown to look rather like a large, fierce old tomcat. His short temper is best controlled by his wife, who devotes herself to domesticity and her children and grandchildren.

Bart: the Contracts Manager. Bart, 40, is an engineering graduate with a 2:1 degree, and an Associate Member of the Institute of Mechanical Engineers. For practical purposes, he has greatly extended his range of knowledge. His job is to oversee all the operations undertaken by the company. Therefore, he has to combine technical skills and understanding with financial and personnel management, as well as exercise considerable diplomatic skills in his relations with customers. His interests are sport (he is a keen sailor), his family (he is a devoted father of young children) and his work, in which he takes enormous pride, identifying himself totally with each project. He is also an excellent pianist and takes an active part in church affairs, often stepping in as relief organist. His wife is a doctor, working in a children's clinic. She too is an enthusiastic small-boat sailor, and enjoys reading and playing bridge.

Janet: director with special responsibility for design and development. Janet, 35, is the most senior of the three in terms of Process Engineering's hierarchy, being the only child of the Chairman and founder of the company. She has an excellent first degree in biochemistry, plus a Master's degree in Management Studies with special reference to the economic aspects of the subject. She is now single and lives with her parents, spoilt, it is said, by both of them. Always formally courteous, she is really very shy. Although not uninterested in men, she finds emotional commitments difficult – perhaps because at the age of 22 she entered upon a marriage that was wrong from the start and ended within three years. Professionally, she is exceptionally gifted and has led the company forward into the development of new and very competitive products. Her interests are limited to her work and to chess, in which she is of championship standard.

The Applicants

The three candidates are:

Dorothy She is 28 and holds a good honours degree in Business Administration. After obtaining her degree she undertook a Purchasing and Supply course and holds the diploma of the appropriate institute. She is currently employed in the buying office of a large metal stockholders. Her duties include the expediting of supplies from the producers to the users. Dorothy is a fluent and effective oral communicator but does little by way of correspondence. She is married with two children, who are cared for by her widowed mother. Her husband is a senior official in the local rates office.

Alex He is 29, and has a Higher National Certificate in Production Engineering. Since leaving school with 5 'O' levels, he has been working in engineering, initially as a draughtsman. He is not very mathematically minded and never really enjoyed the scientific and numerical aspects of engineering, so he was pleased to be offered a post as a technical representative for his firm, selling its range of pumps and valves to contractors and users. He is a little unhappy about the way in which a senior sales post within his present company was awarded, not on the basis of proven success but to a family connection who had never worked for the company. Disillusioned, he is seeking another job. He is married, his wife is a nurse and they have two young children. He is interested in music and is a keen trumpet player. He is also fond of sea fishing.

Roland He is 26 and has a fine record of study, having obtained an upper second-class degree in Business Studies and a diploma in Purchasing and Supply. He is currently concluding his studies for a Master's degree; this has involved close investigation of the problems of purchasing and supply. He now wishes to enter upon a proper salaried job, having lived for what seems a long time on grants, freelance work and parental support. Elegantly mannered when necessary, he more usually displays an extreme directness and candour, striking straight to the heart of any problem. His powers of written communication have been tested only in the writing of academic reports and dissertations. He is unmarried and lives with his parents. As a hobby he devises computer games, which he sometimes sells to software firms.

The Case Studies

Reports on the Applicants

Confidential reports have been obtained in respect of each candidate. All are said to be honest, trustworthy and hard-working, and their various claims to qualifications have been verified. The following comments were made in testimonials and reports.

Dorothy (a confidential report made to the Chairman by his friend, the chairman of the company for which Dorothy works)

> ... This lady has a very highly organized and precise way of working, showing great attention to detail. She is generally popular with her colleagues but rather lacks tolerance for those less quick-witted than herself. Her duties concentrate on a range of ferrous products, plate, bar, sections and the like. She is liked by customers because of her insistence, usually successful, upon the company's honouring all promises made. We should miss her!

Alex (from a previous employer)

> ... Intellectually, this man is above average without being really original or creative. His strengths are his communication skills, the excellent relationships that his pleasing and helpful character produces and the unwearying diligence he displays. His practical skills are superior to his theoretical knowledge and he would, had be stayed with the company, have been considered for the post of Assistant Works Manager. He is an ingenious man and hates to be defeated by a practical problem. He should do well in such a post as you are offering.

Roland (from his professor)

> ... He is a brilliant student who, if he were less anxious to embark upon an industrial career, could have found a place in research. He has proved a very stimulating personality, with the power to penetrate directly to the heart of intellectual problems. On the occasions when he has appeared at conferences, his diplomatic skills have pleasantly surprised his tutors. It is not possible to comment on his skills in written communications of a business kind since he has been involved mainly in the production of essays, reports and dissertations, all of which have been models of clarity and accuracy. Frankly, I cannot comment with any certainty on his suitability for your post, which must, I feel, be suit-

Process Engineering PLC

able only as a stepping stone and a means of gaining practical industrial experience. I only wish we could offer him a research appointment, but financial stringency forbids! I am sure that he would have original ideas for you.

The Interviewers' Quandary

The interviewing panel meets and interviews the candidates, who have previously been taken on a tour of the company's offices and workshops, and been introduced to senior and middle managers. These senior staff were invited to give their views on the suitability of the candidates, and, expressed numerically, the 'favourable votes' are as follows:

> Dorothy – 2 (given by Buying and Accounts)
> Alex – 3 (Design, Construction and Sales)
> Roland – 3 (Design, Buying and Accounts)

The candidates all interviewed well in terms of manner and self-presentation.

When the results of the interviews and the confidential reports are considered, Nigel argues strongly for Alex on the grounds of practical experience: 'He'll get on OK with our suppliers.' Bart argues strongly for Roland: 'Do let's have a trained mind, someone who hasn't given up his studies. He may not be an engineer, but at least he's got some brains and they can be employed to our advantage – this company's getting short on intellectual power.'

Janet hesitates, then finally places the candidates in this order:

1. Roland 'He has proven mental ability, interviewed well, has the manner and style to suit every occasion and can clearly learn quickly.'
2. Alex 'A good middle-of-the-road man – but do we need that?'
3. Dorothy 'A very nice, intelligent woman – if we had a vacancy in Buying she'd be excellent.'

A frank, informal discussion ensues, with Nigel arguing so strongly for Alex that Bart begins to waver. The decision becomes difficult.

The candidates are re-interviewed; at this time Dorothy withdraws her application because she feels she does not have sufficient technical knowledge.

Janet questions Roland on his technical knowledge and his answers reveal a surprising understanding of engineering processes, although his answers to follow-up questions by Nigel make it clear that this knowledge is a matter of observation rather than practice – as might be expected.

By now Nigel and Janet alone are clear in their choice, with Bart wavering. He argues for a re-advertisement, an idea rejected by Janet on the grounds that there is insufficient time. Suddenly Janet makes up her mind. 'We'll have Roland – at least he has powers to be developed.' Roland is called in and offered the post, which he accepts.

The Outcome

Having started work, Roland pleases the technical staff by his quickness of mind. Site staff vary in their views. Some seek to support him while simultaneously using his lack of practical experience as a means of controlling him. Others regard him as too clever by half but with no 'real' (as they put it) knowledge of industry: 'It's all book stuff.'

Suppliers' responses vary, but in general the older and more experienced works managers and production directors seem to regard him as 'too theoretical'. Moreover, he is relatively easy to sidetrack with discussions of 'insuperable' problems, problems to which his predecessor would have produced either solutions the suppliers could not ignore or discreet threats that would have alarmed them.

However, the debate as to whether Roland can be developed into an efficient External Progress Officer is replaced by another problem. His former professor offers him a university appointment in research, and he resigns after nine months' service.

In haste an approach is made to Alex, but by now he has been offered a sales manager's position with a firm marketing products with which he is familiar.

At this point a new advertisement is issued and the whole process begins again.

Reference section

The selection of staff is probably the most difficult task undertaken by management – and the one containing the greatest element of chance. For there to be even the smallest possibility of success, it is necessary to:

- determine as accurately as is feasible what knowledge, experience, expertise and personal qualities are required in the job;
- decide whether, in the event of a candidate who has much to commend him or her but not fulfilling all the criteria being the only possible choice, one or more of the criteria can be discarded or the job should be re-advertised.

Issues such as these should be discussed and decided in principle before the selection process begins, otherwise hasty and ill-considered solutions may be arrived at and wrong choices made or a candidate of great merit discarded.

The choice of selection methods is critical. In practice, simulation exercises that test candidates' abilities are extremely hard to devise, as well as costly. Despite the difficulties, some thought should be given to devising problems that can be put to candidates, perhaps either as case studies on which they can be questioned or as practical tests.

The composition of the panel making the selection is equally important. Those who compose it should recognize how difficult it will be for them to escape from their own social, intellectual, racial, sexual and visual prejudices, which sometimes arise from the very qualities or experience that have caused them to be chosen as selectors.

It is also necessary to remember that some people have the ability to present themselves favourably at interviews, but, when appointed, prove unsuitable. Most experienced senior managers can relate horrifying stories of disasters of this kind.

The Case Studies

In this case study it seems that:

- the company has not really decided, despite the advertisement, what kind of candidate is preferred;
- faced with candidates who do not fully measure up to the specification in the advertisement, the selectors become confused;
- the selectors seem to be selecting and favouring themselves in the persons of the candidates. This may not be wrong, but do they know what they are doing?
- the final selection:
  has rejected the advice of the senior managers' poll;
  has been made by Janet; was that intended?

Certainly the wrong choice was made and those concerned need to ask why. Perhaps one important reason lies in the probability that none of those concerned has ever given any serious thought to the problems of selecting staff, either by reading or by attending a course. There are many such courses available, for example at further education colleges, and organized by trade and professional bodies, and by private enterprise management consultants.

Apart from that, the senior management of this firm needs to engage in (probably lengthy) open discussion about any specific appointment before they get down to interviewing candidates, and to have drawn up a precise statement of their needs, arranged in order of priority and with a clear indication of the point at which re-advertisement (and perhaps reconsideration of the job itself) becomes essential.

3 Far Travel Ltd

'Amidst the snow and ice'

This company is a coach operator of modest size, possessing ten coaches, eight of which are 56-seaters and two are smaller. It is a family firm, and the five directors are Andrew, the Managing Director; his sons, Jack and Harry; his daughter, Jenny; and his wife, Joan, who acts as Finance Director and takes the chair. Jack, Harry and Jenny drive the coaches and Joan is in charge of all accounting, purchasing and office work.

Andrew is a former Royal Corps of Transport warrant officer who believes that the undoubted success of his company is founded on the soldierly qualities of attention to detail, reliability, courtesy and courageous resolution in the face of difficulties. Since infancy, Jack, Harry and Jenny have been inbued with equal determination, while Joan's motherly charm conceals a steely firmness both with suppliers and with those who fail to pay their bills. She is an equally firm holder of the chair at the family board meetings.

Within the district in which Far Travel operates, it is well known for its determination to keep its coaches running under even the most adverse circumstances. The coaches are in constant use and three non-family drivers are also employed. Frank is a close friend of Jack and was invalided out of the RAF; Charlie is an Indian, who doubles as the mechanic when he is not driving; and Gordon, the newest member of the team, with four years' service, is a former bus driver who left because of the shift-working.

During the winter Far Travel coaches are engaged in holiday tours, which are usually undertaken by one of Andrew's sons with Jenny along as a relief driver if the distances between stop-overs are too long. However, much of the winter work consists of day-trips within the UK, including journeys to sporting events and the theatre, as well as the usual special excursions for people going to conferences, exhibitions and the like.

At the time in question the normal pattern of winter working had been especially demanding. Harry with Jenny, and Jack with Frank, were away on winter sports trips to the Continent, leaving Andrew, Charlie and Gordon to cope with the home business, which became extremely busy. To make matters more difficult, Andrew, who could be called on to drive if necessary, fell and broke his wrist, while Charlie was kept busy, in between short trips, on a spate of minor but time-consuming maintenance problems. That left only Gordon free for longer journeys – and Joan, who was always willing to drive the smallest coach, having early in her marriage gained a public service vehicle (PSV) licence.

The weather got steadily colder, and frost and snow began making travel difficult. Warnings of adverse weather conditions were put out by the emergency and police services, and were reported frequently on radio and television, the latter broadcasting the usual pictures of motorways with lines of slow-moving traffic. One of the bookings that Far Travel had taken for this time was for a party of fifty-four people who planned to attend the institution of a young clergyman in his first living some eighty miles away. The journey involved a brief run on city expressways, followed by a motorway journey to within half a mile of the cleric's church and church hall, which were situated on a main road. The journey was arranged to reach the church by 7.30 p.m. and to leave, after a brief reception at the end of the service, by 9.30 p.m.

On the day of the trip the coach was booked to pick up all its passengers at a central point at 5.30 p.m. sharp, thus giving plenty of time for a punctual arrival. In the morning the snow was falling steadily and repeated warnings of delays on the motorway, with reduced speed limits, were broadcast. Andrew at once telephoned the organizers of the trip to explain that a greater margin of time would now be required in view of the weather, and that his coach would need to start at 4.00 p.m. and leave by 9.00 p.m. at the latest. The organizers agreed to this proposal and started ringing round to warn all concerned.

Andrew informed Gordon of the revised time, but the latter expressed his doubt that he would drive in the conditions then prevailing. Andrew restrained his instinctive reactions and, biting his tongue, said that Gordon should report to the garage at 3.30 p.m. and that in the meantime he, Andrew, would inquire about conditions. When Gordon arrived, the snow had almost ceased but it was still extremely cold and there were warnings that vehicles with diesel engines not using winter-grade fuel were breaking down all over the place.

Andrew, using his long-acquired connections with service station attendants and duty sergeants at police stations, as well as with officials of the motoring associations, had gained a clearer picture of the route. Snow, though still falling in places, was by now much reduced. Traffic on the relevant motorways was moving slowly but there were no total hold-ups. Visibility was sufficient to allow travel at the restricted speed of 50 m.p.h. The forecast was for more snow after midnight, with drifting.

As for the coach, the vehicle selected for this run was the best in the fleet, recently serviced and very reliable. Charlie had spent some time draining out the old fuel and replacing it with winter-grade oil to be quite sure that, even if the nine degrees of frost forecast towards midnight came true, there would be no likelihood of a failure in fuel supply.

Gordon arrived at 3.40 p.m. and announced that he would not drive in the conditions prevailing. Persuasion failed, as did anger and threats, and by 3.50 p.m. Charlie offered to drive, but Joan vetoed this, pointing out that, as his wife was expecting her first baby at any moment, he should not be asked to go as he might not get back in time. 'I wouldn't have wanted YOU to do that, Andy,' she remarked.

'Well, I can't go now either. I daren't drive with this wrist,' was his response, 'so what can we do? I don't know how we shall find a driver at this short notice!'

Much to Andrew's horror and indignation, at 4 p.m. Joan had left the garage as the driver, supported in her decision by Charlie. By 12.30 a.m., she was back at the garage, very tired but distinctly triumphant, and with her pockets stuffed with notes – a gift of £25 from the grateful passengers.

The next morning Gordon received a letter by hand; it stated that he had deliberately disobeyed a legitimate instruction that was neither unlawful nor unsafe. The letter pointed out that in a transport undertaking an employer could reasonably expect obedience in such circumstances, and Gordon was accordingly dismissed for gross misconduct.

Soon afterwards, the office of Far Travel received a 'Notice of Appearance' (Form IT3) from the local industrial tribunal.

Reference section

This case study concerns the employer's right to obedience to instructions and whether refusal to obey an instruction constitutes a sufficient cause for immediate dismissal on grounds of gross misconduct. In the incident described an employee has deliberately and knowingly refused to carry out an instruction that seems to be clearly within the employer's authority, and disobedience to which carries the possibility of dismissal. However, an instruction must not involve anything unlawful or unsafe, and it could well be that Gordon will plead that the instruction involved carelessness as to the safety of all concerned, and that this made it necessary for him to disobey it. In the event, everything passed without incident, but the warnings from official bodies might well indicate that there was some truth in Gordon's contention. Moreover, this appears to be the first occasion on which he has refused to carry out an instruction.

The immediate decision to dismiss Gordon on the grounds of gross misconduct cannot be divorced from the natural indignation and distress Andrew felt at being unable to drive himself and then at seeing his wife undertake a task that, although not especially perilous in his view, was certainly very arduous.

An attempt at conciliation through the services of ACAS would seem prudent, since a decision in the firm's favour is not a foregone conclusion. ACAS is an extremely useful organization, and one of its functions is clearly set out in the following extract from *Fair and Unfair Dismissal* (p. 12):

> Once a complaint has been made to an industrial tribunal, but before the hearing takes place, there is an opportunity for the case to be settled by conciliation. Copies of completed application forms and the *Notice of appearance* by the employer are sent by the industrial tribunals to the Advisory, Conciliation and Arbi-

tration Service (ACAS), an independent service, quite separate from the industrial tribunal. Conciliation is carried out by an ACAS officer, who tries to assist in almost every case, either at the request of the applicant and respondent, or on his or her own initiative. The conciliation officer's job is to try to help the respondent and applicant make a voluntary agreement to settle the complaint without it having to go before an industrial tribunal.

4 Heavy Engineering Ltd

'Retire as you should have done!'

This firm has a total labour force of fifty and makes complicated equipment, usually to designs supplied by customers.

Malcolm is 75 years old, fit, active and a master of his trade as a fitter. He has worked for this company for twenty years but never sought promotion, though his opinions on all technical issues are highly respected.

When Malcolm joined the company some unfortunate experiences at another company, which a prolonged strike had virtually destroyed, had caused him to reject trade unionism. He had, in fact, joined the company because at that time it was a non-union shop. However, as time passed his dislike of trade unionism wavered and eventually, under the influence of his son-in-law, his views changed. He became an ardent trade unionist who succeeded in interesting his fellow workers in membership, so that in the end what had been a non-union organization had to not only approve and accept trade unionists but become a closed shop.

These efforts, pursued by Malcolm with the zeal of a convert, have not made him popular with the works management, especially as he is now the works convenor and greatly esteemed in trade-union circles. Of late there have been a number of clashes with management, mainly over pay differentials and working hours, which have included a period of overtime banning and working to rule. In all these events Malcolm has played a leading and aggressive role.

Amongst the work being dealt with is an especially complicated and novel device. Fitting it together has proved exceptionally difficult. On three occasions so far an expensive and highly brittle high-silicon iron sleeve ground precisely internally and externally has been smashed while fitters have been attempting to assemble it into the whole piece of equipment. Of the three breakages, two have

Heavy Engineering Ltd

been made by Malcolm and one by a much younger man, Jack. Each breakage involves considerable expense and considerable delay. So far no sleeve has been fitted.

Four new sleeves have arrived but no sooner have they been unloaded and taken into the assembly bay than a dispute breaks out between the management and fitters over what the latter feel is their unfair treatment. It has become known that some semi-skilled borers, using machines that they cannot set up for themselves, are earning considerably more money than the fitters. The fitters, led by Malcolm, demand parity with the borers: 'We're skilled men, we work just as long, and our work is heavy.'

The Works Manager, Garry, is becoming increasingly peevish. The Technical Sales Manager is grumbling to him that his customer is vexed by the assembly delays resulting from the sleeve breakages, and now there is, Garry feels, a deliberate 'go-slow' engineered, he thinks, by Malcolm. As all this tension is in the air, an attempt is made to fit the newly arrived sleeves.

Malcolm is engaged in a heated discussion with Garry as the younger fitter succeeds for the first time in fitting one of the sleeves. Malcolm and Garry appear ashen and red-faced with anger, respectively, and the men in the shop hear Garry say, 'I wish you'd retired when you should have done. You were good once – now your bloody trade unionism has ruined you and will ruin the company!'

Malcolm picks up a sleeve and starts to fit it. His concentration has gone and he promptly breaks it.

'Now that proves it!' cries Garry. 'You'll have to go. Retire as you should have done ten years ago! You can't concentrate because your mind is on other things. Don't do another. Just leave it to Jack!'

The next morning Malcolm receives a letter of dismissal on the grounds that he is past retirement age and physically unable to do the work. Ironically, by this time Jack has smashed two more of the sleeves, and the customer's and the company's chief draughtsmen are in conference by telephone on the inherent problems of the design.

Malcolm is very angry indeed and seeks advice from his union's regional office. In one sense the Regional Officer is inclined to the view that Malcolm should retire to allow a younger man have the job but, on the other hand, he feels that the company may have acted unfairly and in a way prejudicial to the union. The same thought has occurred to the Managing Director, but Garry says that there is no danger 'because you can't plead unfair dismissal when you're over 65'.

Reference section

Garry has not given the correct information to the Managing Director. It is true that in general people over 65 are unable to complain of unfair dismissal. However, as *Individual Rights of Employees* (p. 18) makes clear, 'There is no qualifying period of employment or age limit for those complaining that they have been unfairly dismissed because of their trade union membership or activities.' The same rule applies to those complaining of sexual or racial discrimination.

Malcolm's record of breakages could point to an inability to carry out his work were it not for the fact that the younger fitter's record of breakages is eventually as bad as Malcolm's, although he alone succeeded in fitting one correctly. Nevertheless, the fact that the two chief draughtsmen are in conference points to the existence of a design problem. Finally, of course, Garry's remarks in the presence of witnesses could be used to argue that the real cause of dismissal was Malcolm's union activities.

Over the whole story there hangs an air of worsening relationships between management and employees, and the failure of those responsible to perceive that pay differentials that seem unjust are a principal cause of dispute. In this instance there has already been trouble involving skilled and semi-skilled employees. Skilled personnel are almost always suspicious of pay differentials that place them at a disadvantage on what appears to be a permanent basis. When this situation arises, management must take restorative action or face trouble.

Reconciliation seems desirable before more serious industrial action is taken. Perhaps ACAS could help (see p. 38 for a description of its conciliatory function).

5   Scraps & Scrap Ltd

'Look, I can swing it like a yo-yo!'

You are the principal shareholder and chairman of this private limited company. It is a small scrap-dealer's business employing only twenty-five people, some in the yard, some collecting and delivering, and some in the office.

Until recently Gavin was employed in the yard, but he was dismissed by you. Gavin is, in a confused way, resentful and bitter, and you are feeling very angry. The circumstances of the dismissal were these.

Your scrap-yard deals with all kinds of scrap but a principal source of material is 'written-off' motor vehicles, mainly private cars. When all reusable parts have been removed and sorted for resale in the warehouse attached to the yard, the shell of the vehicle is picked up by a grab and placed in a crusher, which converts it into a neat, solid metal cube.

Gavin used to operate the grab. You employed him from the time he left the merchant navy and felt sympathetic towards him because he had served in the Falklands campaign. However, you soon discovered that without the strict supervision he had enjoyed at sea Gavin was, in fact, a man with a serious alcohol problem. He normally consumed 6 to 8 pints of beer at midday and a considerably greater quantity in the evening.

At first he seemed to be able to cope with the job, but latterly the drinking began to tell on him. There were near-accidents and his mates regarded him with suspicion and alarm. This eventually caused you to warn him, in the presence of the yard foreman, that further errors could lead to his dismissal. It was an unhappy occasion and one that upset you because, after some initial bluster, this large, red-faced man began to weep. He promised to reform.

Before long, however, the foreman reported that the other workers were complaining about Gavin, and you gave him a written warning. The final incident occurred when Gavin, wildly excited, had deliberately begun to swing a large car body held in the grab to and fro, shouting with amusement and threatening to drop it on people in the yard. Before the foreman could climb into the cab of the crane Gavin had dropped the car, fortunately missing any living creature but wrecking your own almost-new car.

Gavin sat slumped in the crane cab. While he was being removed your secretary typed a brief letter stating that he was dismissed instantly for gross misconduct following a warning of the consequences of further acts of that kind. In an angry scene you told the befuddled Gavin of his dismissal and thrust the letter into his pocket. The confused and resisting man was then escorted from the yard and the gates closed. After a few kicks and shouts he was seen staggering down the street. That afternoon his wages to date and his P45 form were sent to him by registered post.

About a week later you receive a letter, obviously not actually written by Gavin but signed by him in his rather scrawling hand. It claims that he has been unfairly dismissed, stating that as he never had any written statement of his conditions of employment nor any notice of disciplinary and grievance procedures as required by law, he was unaware of them. The letter, clearly written by someone with knowledge of the law, then threatens an approach to an industrial tribunal.

Reference section

Whoever wrote the letter for Gavin had done what you should have done, namely read the booklet *Written Statement of Main Terms and Conditions of Employment*, which is based on the Employment Protection (Consolidation) Act 1978, as amended by the Employment Act 1982. It explains that within thirteen weeks of an employee starting work he or she must be given a written statement of the main hours of employment and an additional note of disciplinary and grievance procedures. The booklet lists all the points that should be mentioned and provides an example of such a statement. It also explains that an employee who has not received such written particulars may refer to an industrial tribunal.

You need to study this booklet, especially as you appear to have failed to comply with the law, perhaps for all your employees. There is no penalty for failure to supply written terms of employment, but should the case go before a tribunal time will be wasted as they are spelt out.

As for Gavin's threat to plead unfair dismissal before an industrial tribunal, it is likely that a tribunal would be strongly influenced in your favour by Gavin's flagrant and dangerous misconduct, not only on the one occasion but on previous occasions, and the fact that you had given him both an oral and a written warning. Moreover, it could be that Gavin's medical condition – that is, if he is an alcoholic – could have given grounds for dismissal earlier. The booklet *Fair and Unfair Dismissal* gives the following guidance:

> **Dismissal in connection with illness**
> The inability of an employee to do a job, for whatever reason, is a valid reason for dismissal. However, the case of the employee who becomes physically or mentally unable to do his or her job because of illness, or is persistently absent from work because of illness, clearly demands special consideration. Tribunals recognize that – especially in the smaller firm – it will often not be possible for the organization to 'carry' the ill employee, and they understand that a time comes when the employer can no longer be expected to keep open the post of an employee who is off sick.
>
> As with dismissals for other reasons, however, they expect the employer to have discussed the position with the employee concerned and to be absolutely sure of the facts about the employee's state of health and whether he or she is incapable of doing his or her job, or likely to be persistently absent in the future. This may involve taking medical advice about the employee's condition by talking, with the employee's permission, to his or her doctor. If there is less demanding work available which the sick employee would be capable of doing, the tribunal will normally expect the employer to offer it to the employee.

Perhaps a prudent management should have seen the problem and its attendant dangers coming and tried to help Gavin as an ethical duty.

6 Auto Processing Ltd

'I couldn't do nothing, could I?'

This small firm is engaged in the design, manufacture and installation of specialized plant for industries producing pastes and polishes. It employs fifty people plus specially contracted labour.

Rodney is an installation foreman responsible for site work and in charge of a gang of six men. The work requires a considerable degree of fitting skill and careful supervision since the equipment is equipped with complicated electrical circuits as well as complex mechanical systems. Malfunction of the equipment can be both expensive and embarrassing to the manufacturer.

At the time of the incident the company is engaged in erecting equipment for a firm producing a polish that is supplied in tins in a variety of colours. The introduction of a new range of polishes makes the rapid and successful installation of the machinery a matter of urgency. When the installation is finished, the manufacturer gives it a trial run and the installation gang leaves the site.

Five weeks later the polish manufacturer's Production Director telephones in a fury, demanding a large sum in compensation for what he describes as 'a total, embarrassing and costly disaster'. Apparently, the polish has begun to 'ferment' in the tins at the retailers, forcing open the lids and running down to damage other stock. The cause has been traced to an incorrectly installed device that failed gradually over the five-week period. In the course of this acrimonious conversation the Production Director says, 'It might never have occurred had your foreman not deserted his post and left the gang alone for a day!'

This is news to the company's Installation Manager: no such information had reached him nor had Rodney requested any leave. He makes immediate inquiries and discovers that Rodney was indeed absent for one entire day at a crucial stage of the installation, having entrusted the job to a technically qualified but much less experienced assistant.

Rodney is at that time at the firm's HQ and is sent for immediately. He does not deny the accusation that he was absent. At this point the Production Director, who has taken over the matter from Rodney's immediate superior, the Installation Manager, says curtly, 'I want to hear nothing more. Don't say another word. You are dismissed from this moment. Your gross misconduct and total dereliction of duty is a breach of the terms and conditions of your employment and will cost the company thousands of pounds as well as loss of reputation. Leave at once and don't come back!'

With that the Production Director leaves Rodney standing and, taking the Installation Manager with him, goes to visit the injured customer. On his way out he tells his secretary to instruct the wages office to pay Rodney his money to date and hand him his P45 with a written confirmation of dismissal and the reason for it.

Rodney gets home in some agitation and writes a letter asking to be allowed to offer an explanation. He receives a reply to the effect that the decision to dismiss him is final and will not be revoked.

The facts of the explanation Rodney wished to make concern his dissolved marriage. He and his ex-wife have remained friendly and always kept in touch. She lives near the site of the installation and on arriving there Rodney received a message from her that she had been badly injured in a road accident and was in hospital. As a result, her rather isolated house had been left unoccupied and her chickens were without food or drink in very cold, frosty weather. Knowing that Rodney was working within twenty-five miles distance, she was asking him to arrange for the care of her chickens, and turn off and drain the heating and hot water systems.

Rodney knew that any injury to the birds would cause his former wife the utmost distress, so he had hastened to do as she asked. The task took longer than he had expected since he had difficulty in finding someone to feed the chickens. When he returned to the site, he could not see anything wrong (the fault in installation would not have been visible) and received an assurance that no trouble or difficulties had been experienced.

Reference section

Rodney's action was undoubtedly rash and he appears not to have given any thought to its possible consequences. On the other hand, the presence of a technically knowledgeable assistant and the belief that he would accomplish his mission quickly makes Rodney's absence rather less serious.

There are definitely substantial grounds for dismissing him, but the company are in error in not giving Rodney an opportunity to state his case and defend himself, perhaps by pointing out that it was in the agony of the moment that he failed to inform a superior. Failure to provide that opportunity is certainly contrary to the ACAS guidelines on the essentials of good procedure: 'The employer should always give the employee a proper opportunity to put his or her side of the case even in a case of gross misconduct and should take account of what the employee says *before making any decision* about dismissal' (*Fair and Unfair Dismissal*, p. 9). Failure to adopt a proper and fair procedure can affect any compensation awarded.

If Rodney takes his case to an industrial tribunal, a decision against his claim that he has been unfairly dismissed is by no means certain. A tribunal would consider whether dismissal was within the band of reasonable responses by a reasonable employer.

The case study makes clear the need for drawing up and carrying out fair and proper procedures binding on all concerned. Such procedures, outlined in the ACAS code of practice, help managers in moments of crisis to avoid impetuous actions that may afterwards be successfully challenged. Have Auto Processing drawn up such procedures? If not, they should seek the advice of ACAS and in the meantime study pp. 27-32 of *Fair and Unfair Dismissal*, which deal with the ACAS code.

7 Goldwares Ltd

'It was just a mistake'

Goldwares Ltd manufactures jewellery using precious metals, principally gold and silver. It is rather old-fashioned firm operating in a group of old, converted dwelling houses with numerous stairways, passages and workshops of various sizes. In order to satisfy fire regulations the premises have no fewer than four exits. The doors on three of them are marked 'Emergency Exit Only', but, in practice, these are continually used in order to avoid climbing up and down internal staircases and traversing various workshops. Because of the value of the articles produced much stress is laid upon security, but there are really no serious checks on employees.

Although a small firm, relations between staff are not entirely harmonious. Normally, any difficulties are moderated partly by the physical nature of the environment, which tends to keep people apart, and partly by the fact that the organization of work results in the formation of self-contained groups.

The owners of the company, who emigrated from Hong Kong many years ago, pride themselves on the high quality of the work and have been able to maintain the standard despite the large volume of goods produced. They contend that an important factor in their success has been that they have avoided a great deal of the subcontracting common to the trade by carrying out virtually all processes on their own premises.

One particularly important process is finishing and polishing. This workshop has a foreman, Tom, and four polishers, Neil, Bert, Graham and Mohamet. Tom is a cantankerous veteran, aged 70, with forty years' experience with this company. He is not given to suffering fools gladly, and has been retained past retirement age because, difficult though he can be, he has an enviable record of product quality. Tom's squad tend to regard themselves, under his guidance, as an élite, who, to quote Tom, 'put right other people's bad workmanship'.

Neil, 36, is the senior polisher, with ten years' service and an unblemished character.

The section concerned with making rings has as its head an ambitious young man, John, not noted for good nature or tolerance. He has already had numerous brushes with Tom and has been heard to refer to him as a 'drunken old dodderer, a relic of the Dark Ages!'

The Works Manager, Calvin, is also a comparatively young man, and is John's brother-in-law. He believes he has the task of dragging the firm into the twentieth century, although, judging by the balance sheets, it is highly profitable regardless of which century it appears to be in.

One of the ways in which Tom maintains the loyalty of his team is by his refusal to accept any need for decisions about staff privileges and absences to be taken by anyone but himself. Therefore, he rarely discusses such matters with Calvin and there are frequent grumbles that 'Tom's lads' do as they like.

This does not please Calvin, who regards the polishing shop as a rebellious group determined to undermine his authority. However, the situation remains unchanged and complaints to the Chairman and General Manager meet with a response that Calvin finds extremely annoying: 'Look, Tom's a good old chap really and knows the job. Just be patient and one day he'll retire and then you'll have a real problem – how to maintain his standards!'

One morning in winter Neil receives a telephone message that his aged father has been taken ill and is to go to hospital that day. Neil's father lives some forty miles away. He is a widower and his sole companion is a large, short-tempered dog. Neil and his wife, Janet, live some five miles from the factory. Janet once worked in the office at Goldwares, but now works in a jeweller's shop and is currently on maternity leave.

On receiving the telephone message, Neil approaches Tom and requests permission to go at once to see that his father is safely in hospital and to take care of the dog. He is highly agitated and distressed. 'Off you go, lad' is Tom's response. Whereupon, still wearing his brown overall coat, which all employees buy for themselves,

Goldwares Ltd

Neil rushes out by a back stairway through an emergency door to his car and drives off.

Not long afterwards heavy snow falls on the region, making movement difficult. No message is received from Neil the next morning. At this point, John arrives in the polishers' shop demanding some rings. Tom is not back from lunch and John also discovers that Neil is absent.

Determined to create a situation of maximum embarrassment, John, without more ado, drives to Neil's house. Finding Janet in, he has little difficulty in discovering that Neil has not returned. John notices Neil's overall coat in the hall and, picking it up, feels the presence of rings in one of the pockets. Telling Janet 'I'll take this', he leaves at once and returns to the works.

Back at Goldwares John goes immediately to Calvin, shows him the unpolished rings discovered in the pocket and suggests Neil's immediate dismissal on the grounds of gross misconduct. He points out that the written terms of employment provided by the company and the note on disciplinary and grievance proceedings make clear that the penalty for dishonesty and any breach of security rules is summary dismissal.

Tom, now returned from lunch and smelling, as always, of beer but perfectly sober in manner, is summoned. He receives a severe admonishment and warning for what Calvin declares is a serious breach of factory discipline and security, coupled with a suggestion that he had probably intended to conceal Neil's absence and thus ensure no deduction in pay or loss of annual leave.

Later that day Neil returns, having struggled through the snow. He is at once brought before Calvin and summarily dismissed for gross misconduct. His dismissal is accompanied by a suggestion that he should more correctly be accused of theft. His efforts to explain are shouted down.

The next morning the Chairman receives a visit from the factory shop steward, whom he seldom encounters in his official capacity since industrial disputes have been rare. Without wasting time, the shop steward asks, in tones far removed from his customary friendliness, if the Chairman is aware of Neil's dismissal and if he had read the ACAS Code of Practice on disciplinary practice and procedures in employment. He says that a very serious mistake has been made and that a preliminary discussion with the legal staff of the union makes it probable that unless appropriate action is taken at once a hearing before an industrial tribunal will be arranged.

Reference section

Here is a typical instance, albeit somewhat dramatic, of the way in which unresolved personal and procedural issues can, without warning, result in serious problems. The issues that need to be investigated and resolved in this case include:

- whether Neil committed an act of 'gross misconduct';
- the causes of the bad relations between Tom and John;
- the causes of the bad relations between Tom and Calvin;
- the apparent inability of the organization to provide proper security procedures;
- the fact that the formal and informal procedures clearly are too far apart;
- the readiness of both John and Calvin to ignore the correct disciplinary procedures in pursuit of what appear to be personal dislikes and internal politics;
- the possible absence of any understanding of contemporary employment legislation – bad in John and potentially disastrous in Calvin, as the Works Manager.

The booklet *Fair and Unfair Dismissal* requires thorough reading, especially 'Appendix II – ACAS Code of Practice'.

It is necessary for the Chairman to consider as a matter of urgency any explanation that Neil wishes to offer for the presence off the firm's premises of articles of value found in his overall pocket; so far Neil has not been allowed to make an explanation. There is good reason to suppose that what happened was the ill-considered action of a distressed and worried man, and that his action, though wrong, was one of negligence rather than gross misconduct. Failure to allow an employee to provide an explanation for his conduct is looked on with disfavour by industrial tribunals.

In this case the tribunal would consider: (i) whether the employer believed that the rings had been stolen; (ii) whether the employer had reasonable grounds to sustain that belief; and (iii) whether, at the time the employer formed that belief on those grounds, he had carried out a reasonable investigation of the circumstances. If there is an appeal, then the tribunal will have to consider any further facts, either procedural or concerning the actual events which come to light.

In general, careful thought needs to be given to setting up, and distributing to all concerned, internal procedures that, while maintaining the dignity and authority of department heads, ensure that information is available centrally and that some decisions are reserved for senior management.

Finally, are the Directors considering the poor relationships currently existing and devoting enough of their time to supervision and reconciliation? Delegation without supervision and control procedures that will reveal failures and growing problems is as dangerous as over-centralization.

8 The International

'Over-seasoning'

You and your partner own a private limited company running a very superior restaurant, which appears with numerous 'stars' in all the guides, attesting to its very high standard of food and service.

The management of the restaurant is in the hands of well-paid senior staff. The Manager is in overall charge, but he is on holiday. In the dining room all day-to-day management, including engagement and dismissal of staff, is entrusted to the head waiter, an employee of five years' standing. In the restaurant he is always known as Monsieur Louis, but, in fact, he comes from Huddersfield, not France, and his real name is James Smith. He has a very good grasp of what may be described as 'restaurant French', which, coupled with a carefully polished style, proves most impressive to the restaurant clientele. He has been well trained, is very experienced, and is an excellent head waiter with one serious exception: his extraordinary suavity of manner towards the clientele and his desire to please them is not reflected in his behaviour towards the staff. Out of hearing of the guests the French style and accent disappear and M. Louis is transformed into the extremely brusque and sometimes abusive James.

However, an abrasive style is part of life at your restaurant. The chef, Heinrich, is a German of great culinary brilliance, but one who cultivates a prima donna style to the utmost. Indeed, were it not for the constant flow of well-trained young people seeking to gain experience and reputation by working at so famous an establishment, the business would grind to a close. As it is, the superlative food, the elegant decor and the excellence of the service conceals from the guests the turmoil behind the scenes. In the kitchen the currency of abusive language has been steadily reduced in value by constant repetition, with the result that only occasionally is any deep resentment felt or a severe wound inflicted. Unfortunately, such an occasion has now occurred.

Some six years ago the previous head waiter engaged a waiter named Francis on the recommendation of a wealthy and valued American client of the restaurant. The continued loyalty of the wealthy man was encouraged by this and he has always asked to be served by Francis.

Francis, who is black, is a grave and dignified person. He is courteous, understands food and wines, and rarely makes any mistakes. In James's eyes, however, he has a serious failing – he is too slow. To some extent this is true. Francis is slow and deliberate, but some guests prefer his slowness and manner to the mixture of suavity and speed encouraged by James.

The crisis occurs when, either by chance or by deliberate malice, James places a group of noisy, impatient and slightly intoxicated young men at Francis's table. Before long they are calling and snapping their fingers, grumbling loudly at the service to the point when James, in a burst of carefully concealed rage, dismisses Francis from the dining room and, with the aid of his assistant, personally serves the members of the party, who finally leave, having refused to pay the service charge on the bill.

Shortly afterwards there is a violent scene when James upbraids Francis in the most abusive terms, the final words being '. . . why I have continued to tolerate such an idle, dim-witted, incompetent black bastard in my restaurant for so long is beyond me. Get out of my sight – you're not fit to wait here!'

Francis does exactly as he is told. He does not return for work the next day and James sends you a note that Francis has left without giving any warning of his intention.

Despite his simple and slow manner, Francis is an intelligent man, and he has been deeply wounded by James's words and attitude. He knows there is one powerful, independent person to whom he can turn for advice, and he seeks an interview with the rich American at his office. With his usual dignity Francis tells the man the entire story.

The next day you receive a letter from your American customer explaining what has occurred. He fears that, unbeknown to you, an

56 *The Case Studies*

injustice has been done in forcing Francis to leave and hopes that you will be able to resolve the situation. If this is not possible, then he feels he must suggest to Francis that he should seek legal advice and will be obliged to assist him to do so.

You are endeavouring to digest this information when there is a thunderous knock on your door and Heinrich enters, his face distorted with rage, to announce his immediate departure. 'I will not', he shouts, 'endure any more of the insolence of that brutish phoney Frenchman! I will not suffer him to call me a Nazi swine! I am not a fascist. It is he who is a fascist, a true fascist, brutal and cruel – Francis is a decent man and what does he say to him? Well, he will not abuse me!' With those words he rushes out and seconds later can be seen driving off.

Your immediate concern is to ensure that the guests are treated as always, and in this you are aided by the fact that the various senior but subordinate chefs are all anxious to take over. However, all the staff are united in declining to work if James continues in his job. To gain time you summon James and give him a written notice that he is suspended on full pay while various issues are investigated.

That night the dinner is of excellent quality, and the service under the control of the assistant head waiter is admirable. The next day, you and your partner sit down to take stock of the situation.

Reference section

Your problem divides into two quite distinct issues. The first concerns Francis. Has he merely resigned without giving notice or has he suffered constructive dismissal, which may, in fact, be unfair?

It is true that a certain amount of clearly expressed criticism should be accepted as part of the normal give and take of relations between employer and employee. In this instance you have delegated full power of engagement and dismissal of dining-room staff to your head waiter. In the dining room and in the kitchen a very robust style of language has, by established practice and custom, become normal and acceptable to those employed, although a stranger might find it intolerable.

The following questions need to be answered.

- Did the words used by the head waiter make a breach in the mutual trust and confidence between employer and employee that are implied in the terms of contract, and so result in constructive dismissal?
- Were the words used such as to indicate immediate dismissal?
- Was the phrase 'black bastard', indicating racialism, accompanied by other acts that were discriminatory?

To aid your thinking on this matter you should read *Fair and Unfair Dismissal*. The following extract is from p. 17.

> **Constructive dismissal**
> A tribunal may rule that an employee who resigns because of conduct by his or her employer has been 'constructively dismissed'. For a tribunal to rule in this way the employer's action has to be such that it can be regarded as a substantial breach of the employment contract indicating that he or she intends no longer to be bound by the contract: an example of this might be where the employer arbitrarily demotes an employee to a lower rank or poorer paid position. The contract is what has been agreed between the parties, whether orally or in writing or a combination of both, together with what must necessarily be implied to make the contract workable.

You should also pay particular attention to 'When is dismissal fair or unfair?' (p. 6) and 'What are the elements of good procedure?' (p. 9) in the same booklet.

Although racial abuse is not in itself discrimination, the booklet *Racial Discrimination – a Guide to the Race Relations Act 1976* (p. 8) makes clear that 'It is . . . unlawful for an employer to discriminate by dismissing an employee or treating him unfavourably in any other way.' You should read this booklet and the Commission for Racial Equality's *Code of Practice*.

You will, of course, need to obtain a full and clear account of the events leading up to Francis's departure by taking statements from witnesses and those concerned.

In addition to the problem of Francis you have to deal with Heinrich's resignation and departure without notice, and James's suspension. You may consider that Heinrich, who was in no way subordinate to James, has voluntarily resigned without having referred his grievance to you in the absence of the Manager, although you may believe his grievance to be a real one. However, although he has not been directly dismissed by you, your partner or the only other person with this authority – the absent Manager – could he claim that some implied terms of contract relating to the behaviour of co-workers have been breached?

You may consider that James has proved to be a source of trouble and disharmony far exceeding any value his talents may have. If this is so, then before you do anything else you have to obtain as clear a view of all the facts as you can. This may well involve many interviews and much trouble.

If it proves that James's abuse of both Francis and Heinrich exceeded all reasonable bounds, then you can consider whether he has been guilty of gross misconduct, warranting summary dismissal, or whether he should be warned – preferably in writing. *Fair and Unfair Dismissal* states:

> **Unsatisfactory conduct of employee**
> Except where the default is so serious as to justify summary dismissal, for example where an employee has been caught 'red-handed' in an act of gross misconduct, an employee should always be told in what way he or she is at fault and warned that an improvement must be made. It is not essential to put warnings in writing, but it is desirable to do so. A written note will ensure that the employer's intentions are absolutely clear and may also be useful in evidence should the case come to a tribunal.
>
> The employee should be given a reasonable time to improve after being warned.

9 Chemcon PLC

'I can't go today!'

Chemcon PLC employs fifty full-time and many casual employees and is engaged in a specialist form of chemical engineering contract work. Each gang it employs usually consists of a number of craftsmen and labourers, a semi-skilled man who prepares the materials and a foreman. At the company headquarters there is a Labour Manager, whose job is normally limited to organizing the deployment of gangs of men to the various sites where the company is fulfilling its contracts. He is also the chief subordinate of the Personnel Manager, for whom he deputizes. The Personnel Manager has no formal qualifications; he is an experienced employee who was formerly the chief clerk in the wages office.

The company's work is frequently concerned with maintenance or reconstruction. In these cases there is always the danger that some continuous process will be disrupted or that a particular piece of plant will be taken out of production for longer than specified, either of which may cause a great deal of disorganization and expense. Therefore, the work of the Labour Manager is of considerable importance, as failure to ensure the proper deployment of labour may cause loss of future contracts and much ill feeling. The site foremen are under pressure to carry out work without any unnecessary interference with production and the correct composition of these gangs is very important to them.

The Labour Manager, Reginald, is in his mid-fifties. He has been with the company since his early twenties, when he joined as a craftsman. After some years as a foreman, at which he was most successful, he was promoted to Labour Manager, a position he has held for fifteen years.

Reginald knows most of the labour force personally, and has worked with most of them either as a fellow craftsman or as a foreman. He is essentially a very old-fashioned man to whom long hours of demanding work seem normal. As a younger man he took pride not only in his considerable craft skill but also in his endurance. When his children were young, his wife stayed at home and he supported the family on his very high earnings, from which they not only purchased a modest, well-situated house but also saved money. He remains conscious that his prosperity has been based upon his loyal service and has never failed to respond to the company's sudden and arbitrary demands.

Much of the site labour is employed on a 'freelance' basis as and when contracts arise. Most of the men have worked for the company for some years and many fill in any slack hours by doing work elsewhere. In fact, the only permanent hourly-paid personnel are some craftsmen, the foremen, the materials-preparation men and those employed at the depot and at the works, where much of the specialized material is prepared. The written terms of employment require everyone to be available for site work.

The craftsmen are all men who have either been promoted from labourer or come to the company with a craft skill that could be used with a modest amount of retraining for the special work done by the company. The semi-skilled materials-preparation men are all trained by the company on promotion from the ranks of the labourers. They tend to be the most stable part of the labour force, and when not out on site, are employed in the depot or at the factory. Foremen are always former craftsmen and are often 'working' foremen, since the gangs are usually no more than four or five in number.

Because of the nature of the work, remuneration for hourly-paid staff is much higher than normal, with virtually guaranteed overtime and large non-taxable payments covering travelling and lodgings expenses. This being so, there is low turnover of personnel, resulting in an unusually high average age for craftsmen and semi-skilled men. These men are, in general, accustomed to sudden demands for their services, constant changes of location and long periods away from home. Given their average age, they are rarely subject to the heavy domestic responsibilities associated with young children.

However, there is one much younger worker among the skilled Lionel is ambitious and able. He is also an unusual employee the last three years he has been continuously engaged in

Chemcon PLC

testing material and carrying out various maintenance jobs in the factory, and has not been employed on site work.

Lionel is married to Greta, who is a senior saleswoman in the model gowns department of a fashionable department store. They have two children, a boy of 2 and a girl of 5. Greta's widowed mother lives nearby and Lionel's parents live about two miles away. Greta takes the children to her mother-in-law early each weekday morning. From there the elder child is taken to school (and later collected) while the younger child is looked after. On the Saturdays when Greta is on duty and Lionel is working overtime at the factory, the children are looked after by Greta's mother, who works as a telephonist during the week.

Difficulties suddenly arise when Lionel's mother has a nasty attack of influenza, and Greta's mother is away on a holiday. This situation coincides with one of the sudden crises that are a normal part of life at the company.

On Thursday afternoon a customer operating a continuous process telephones to ask for immediate help. A reaction vessel lined with special tiles has had to be taken out of service because some tiles have fallen away from their backing, thus exposing the metal to corrosive liquids. The firm has been able to slow down the process and direct part-processed liquids into receivers pending the repair of the reaction vessel's lining.

As soon as the news is received the Construction Manager organizes the loading of the necessary materials, portable plant and tools, and asks Reginald to arrange for a gang of four men, consisting of a working foreman, one craftsman, one labourer and one semi-skilled man, to be dispatched to the customer's premises.

For once Reginald's usual luck deserts him and he has difficulty in collecting a gang together. Whenever he telephones or sends a messenger, he finds that the man is away, otherwise engaged or claiming to be ill. Then he suddenly remembers Lionel. Why not, he reasons, send him? A quick call to the works superintendent is sufficient to persuade him that Lionel can be spared and Lionel is asked to go at once to Reginald's office.

Lionel does, feeling somewhat puzzled. Reginald tells him to report at once to the site, about a hundred miles away. He is to start work on arrival and continue over the weekend on the emergency, and then to stay on for another three days to carry out some non-urgent work that can be conveniently undertaken while the men are there.

Lionel is dismayed by this instruction. He explains that his domestic situation is very complicated at present. His wife is out of town on a special course related to her work and his mother is ill with a severe attack of influenza. His father, a chief steward on the Newcastle-Bergen route, is away at sea and cannot help. He has arranged for one of his mother's neighbours to collect the elder child from school and look after her and his son until he returns from work. He had intended to follow his wife's normal routine on Friday with the neighbour again substituting for his mother, and to look after the children himself on Saturday. His wife will return on Saturday evening.

Lionel explains that by starting late on Saturday or early on Sunday he could probably arrive on site to work on Sunday and could then continue there for the less urgent work. He points out that although originally engaged for contract work, for the past three years he has been continuously employed on a Monday-to-Friday programme of work, earning less money than the contracting staff. He thinks it unfair to make so inconvenient a demand on him.

Reginald, already extremely frustrated by his unsuccessful effort to find men, is enraged. 'Why,' he says, 'you've neither loyalty nor sense! Have you read your contract? Here, it says you're to be mobile – you're in a contracting business. Just because you've had a soft job, it doesn't mean it's forever!'

'I'm sorry, I can't go until late Saturday or early Sunday,' Lionel responds. 'Can't you understand how impossible it is – or perhaps you never had to take care of your children.'

This last observation is a sharper reply than Lionel realizes, since one of Reginald's four sons died in infancy while he was 300 miles away working on an urgent contract.

'I'm not interested in your hard luck story,' Reginald declares. 'All I want to know is, are you going? If not, you're sacked for a gross breach of your contract.'

'I won't go immediately, as I've told you,' Lionel replies.

'Then you will go for good,' says Reginald.

Now it so happens that the Personnel Manager is on holiday and

Chemcon PLC

Reginald is acting for him. Thus it occurs that Lionel receives his dismissal from Reginald. When the Personnel Manager returns from holiday, his first batch of mail contains a 'Notice of Appearance' (Form IT3) from the local industrial tribunal in respect of a complaint of unfair dismissal made by Lionel.

He discusses the matter with Reginald and hears his side of the story. He visits Lionel, whose account of events coincides, with differences in emphasis and phrasing, with Reginald's. Lionel asks the Personnel Manager to reverse the dismissal and is told that further thought must be given before a reversal can be made.

Reference section

The Personnel Manager has to consider what the outcome might be if he does not reinstate Lionel immediately and the case goes to an industrial tribunal.

On the one hand Lionel voluntarily accepted a contract that required him to be mobile and work at locations determined by the demands of the company's business. To that extent, therefore, it might seem that Reginald had a formally correct and legally based reason for dismissing him.

On the other hand, as in all such situations, the question of what is reasonable and fair needs to be considered. There appears to be nothing in Lionel's work record that would indicate that his behaviour was consistently uncooperative, and he has offered a very clear and reasonable explanation for his refusal to leave immediately for the site.

An industrial tribunal will hold to the principle that an employer must not only have a valid reason for dismissing an employee, but also act reasonably. *Fair and Unfair Dismissal* includes the following explanation:

> ### What is reasonable procedure and sufficient reason for dismissing an employee?
> An employer must act reasonably in all the circumstances in treating the reason for dismissing the employee as a sufficient reason for the dismissal. Not only must the employer have a valid reason for the dismissal, but also he or she must have acted reasonably in all the circumstances in dismissing the employee

> for that particular reason. The question whether the employer acted reasonably not only involves consideration of the way in which the dismissal was carried out, but also whether he or she acted reasonably in relation to the situation leading up to the decision to dismiss the employee. For example, if the employee was dismissed for misconduct or lack of capability, it is necessary to consider whether he or she was warned and given a chance to improve . . .

To establish whether the order given was reasonable, the tribunal will consider the terms of the contract between Lionel and the company, whether oral, written or implied, as they relate to hours of work and whether overtime is compulsory. It will also consider whether the order was reasonable in the particular circumstances and therefore take into account Lionel's domestic situation.

Thus, if Lionel's plea that he has been unfairly dismissed goes before the tribunal, the company could be regarded as having acted unreasonably.

To help to decide the action to be taken *Fair and Unfair Dismissal* should be consulted, including 'What is conciliation?' (p. 12).

10 Wiring Work PLC

'He's always been difficult!'

Wiring Work PLC is engaged in electrical wiring contracts which are primarily for outside wiring on large industrial sites. This work involves a great deal of climbing and exposure to adverse weather conditions.

You are the company's newly-appointed Personnel Officer. Your previous job was Secretary/Personal Assistant to the Chairman, who has suddenly decided that a personnel officer is necessary. You are a graduate, but, as an Asian woman, have found some difficulty in obtaining a line-management position. You took your previous job to gain experience.

The staff consists of the usual commercial and financial personnel, buyers, technical sales people, draughtsmen and technical managers. In addition, there are 3 transport drivers, 5 depot and 20 site labourers, 60 installation staff (wiremen), and 8 stores workers.

The stores department supplies the workers on site with their requirements. The stores staff have been recruited down the years through advertisements, personal contact and Jobcentres. Rather unusually, none of them has ever worked on large industrial sites, though some of them have worked on small indoor contracts, both domestic and industrial.

With the exception of Jonathan, all the wiremen are in the mid-twenties to early forties age range. This has come about by chance, as a number of the older men have left to set up small electrical businesses or to join other companies. To date, no wireman has retired from the company.

Jonathan is 52 and has worked with the company for twenty years. He is an extremely experienced man, having been engaged on large-scale contracting work since he completed his apprenticeship. A very able technician and craftsman, he has been entrusted with some supervisory duties from time to time, but has always preferred to avoid responsibility for the work of others and to concentrate on his own tasks.

Jonathan is a gentle-looking man of slight build and a deceptively mild manner – in fact, he has a rather irascible temperament and can be sharply spoken and extremely obstinate when crossed. He is respected for his skills, which he is always willing, in his rather didactic way, to share, but has no close friends amongst his colleagues despite his length of service.

Unfortunately, Jonathan has slowly become more and more arthritic, so that the physical agility and endurance demanded by the job have become beyond him. For a while his obstinate courage has concealed the full extent of his disability, but on a recent job his colleagues had to rescue him from a situation beyond his physical powers and to 'carry' him for the rest of the contract.

This fact has become known to the Contracts Manager, Kevin, a man in his fifties. His breezy manner and bluff, outspoken ways have not appealed to Jonathan, and there have been clashes between them quite out of keeping with their relative positions. Kevin now proposes that Jonathan should be asked to resign, with a promise that the firm will try to find him an indoor post with some other electrical firm.

This proposal is put to Jonathan, who rejects the idea outright. In reply, he suggests that a place be found for him in the stores, where, he claims, his experience will be of value. He has, in fact, made some private inquiries and has discovered that a member of the stores staff, Randolph, is leaving. Randolph is one of two West Indians working in the stores; there are two other West Indian men and two Asian men working on sites. Jonathan concludes his request by saying to Kevin, 'I couldn't do worse than an inexperienced blackie, could I?' This statement is overheard by Kevin's secretary, who repeats it to her boyfriend, an Asian wireman; within a few hours the Stores Manager has heard it too.

The Stores Manager, Francis, is a man of few words, proud of his reputation as a disciplinarian. He attracts the loyalty of his staff by his conviction that no one working for him can possibly be other than in all respects efficient and honest. Partly because of this attitude, there is some tension between the installation men in the field

Wiring Work PLC

and the storemen. When Francis hears of Jonathan's comment, which he regards as insulting to his department, he tells Kevin that he most definitely will not accept the man's transfer.

Normally Kevin would have regarded this rejection as a slight, but as the man in question is Jonathan, he feels himself in agreement with Francis. He therefore suggests that the decision be taken by the General Manager, Robert. Kevin and Francis approach Robert, who is extremely busy with final negotiations for a contract that could guarantee profitable work for five years. Robert's reaction is one of impatience. 'Why bother me?' he asks. 'If, on the one hand, the job is beyond his powers and, on the other, his capacity as a trouble-maker — racist you say, Francis? — is going to cause trouble in the stores, then he must go. Look, I'll phone Cables Incorporated and see if they've some sort of job there.'

Robert does this immediately and finds that a place as a labourer is available. The work is light and Cables Incorporated already have a man with a similar handicap to Jonathan's employed on it.

Armed with Robert's decision and the offer of the job at Cables Incorporated, Kevin approaches Jonathan. He is a little uneasy because he knows the stores position counts as superior semi-skilled work and, although it would produce a gross loss of £30 a week in Jonathan's current wages, the labourer's job would produce not only great loss of status but also a gross loss of £50 a week. None the less, Kevin discharges Jonathan on the grounds that he can no longer perform the work he has been doing and for which he is employed. He recommends that Jonathan does not work his notice but goes at once to Cables Incorporated, where he will be taken on immediately as a labourer. Jonathan points out that he is entitled to substantial notice and Kevin assures him that he will be paid for that period.

Jonathan is extremely angry at his dismissal. He refers the matter to his union and, having left the company, occupies himself not at Cables Incorporated but with the preparing of his case for unfair dismissal for an industrial tribunal.

Your position is a difficult one. Your promotion has not been accompanied by any special training, nor have you had any clear description of your powers. You are, however, now required to provide a report on the whole affair with your recommendations on the position the company should take.

Reference section

Your situation is the kind that occurs more frequently than it should, since you have been given an ill-defined appointment without adequate training. Nevertheless, you have an opportunity to learn some important rules and to provide a clear analysis and sound advice.

The problem that has arisen combines, as is not unusual, ignorance, subjective feeling and haste. Jonathan is clearly not a particularly appealing or popular person, but this does not affect his legal rights.

You should begin by acquiring a basic knowledge of the regulations governing fair and unfair dismissal by reading *Fair and Unfair Dismissal*. In particular, study 'Dismissal in connection with illness', which includes the following statement:

> ... [the tribunals] expect the employer to have discussed the position with the employee concerned and to be absolutely sure of the facts about the employee's state of health and whether he or she is incapable of doing his or her job, or likely to be persistently absent in the future. This may involve taking medical advice about the employee's condition by talking, with the employee's permission, with his or her doctor. If there is less demanding work which the sick employee would be capable of doing, the tribunal will normally expect the employer to offer it to the employee.

It will be noticed at once that the company has not taken any proper formal steps to make sure of the medical facts. General observations, hearsay and the particular occasion referred to in the case study do not provide adequate evidence, although Jonathan's suggestion that a stores job be found for him seems to indicate that he knows that he is no longer fit for outside work.

There is no doubt that if the medical evidence had been clear and incontrovertible, less physically demanding work should, if possible, have been made available. In fact, such work was available in the stores department, but was not offered to Jonathan because of the personal feelings of individual managers and the haste with which the decision to discharge him was taken.

Had Jonathan been offered the stores post and refused it, the situation would have been very much in the firm's favour. If he had taken the job and then behaved in a racist or obstructive manner, there could have been valid reasons for dismissing him. However, his one racist utterance may have been more a matter of insensitivity than of true racial prejudice.

Should the matter go before an industrial tribunal, a decision in Jonathan's favour is a distinct possibility. Therefore, you may well need to recommend some kind of reconciliation, with the help of ACAS or by direct negotiation.

11 Automobiles PLC

'I know he's opinionated, but he's good!'

This company, which began in a small way and has steadily expanded, distributes passenger cars and light commercial vehicles for a major manufacturer, runs a quality used-car business and operates a very efficient service and repair workshop, which handles all makes of vehicle.

The company structure is shown in the diagram on p. 71. The Chairman is very much a figurehead. The management is very simple and rather autocratic in style, the Managing Director's word being 'law'. This is mitigated by a high degree of technical delegation so that, provided the MD's instructions are obeyed, all day-to-day technical and sales activities are delegated to the senior management. There is no Personnel Officer as it is the practice for each director to be his own personnel manager, with the Managing Director taking an active part in all engagements and dismissals.

William, aged 48, is a skilled motor-vehicle mechanic of five years' service. He has an excellent range of qualifications and has undertaken special courses on servicing automatic gearboxes. His standard of work is very high and customers rarely complain about what he has done. His job is section charge-hand and it is for this appointment that he left his previous employer.

In his spare time William studies automatic gearboxes. Although lacking the mathematical and technological skills to advance from practical work to the design of gearboxes, he has a remarkable knowledge of the range of automatic gearboxes available, their various advantages and disadvantages, and the problems of maintenance and repair.

The manufacturer for which Automobiles PLC is a distributor makes an automatic gearbox, which it uses in its own product and sells to other manufacterers. This gearbox is reliable and durable,

Automobiles PLC Company Structure

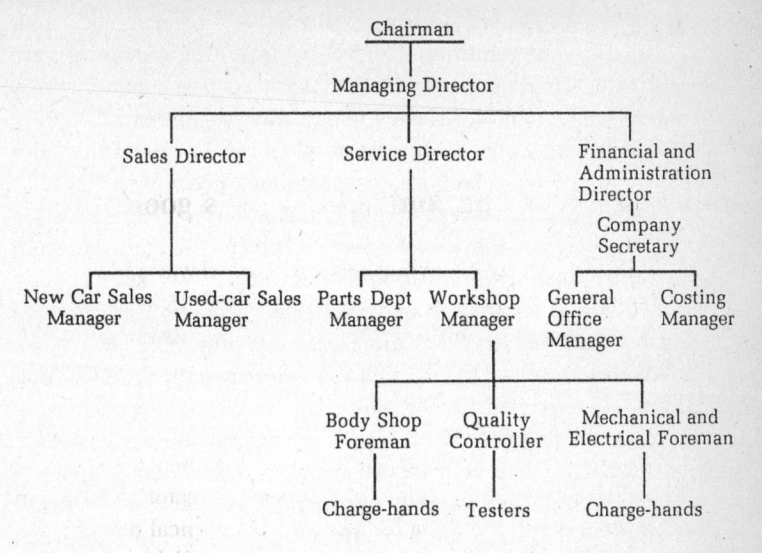

```
                          Chairman
                             |
                    Managing Director
        _____|_____
        |                    |                    |
   Sales Director      Service Director    Financial and
                                           Administration
                                           Director
                                              |
                                           Company
                                           Secretary

New Car Sales  Used-car Sales  Parts Dept  Workshop    General    Costing
Manager        Manager         Manager     Manager     Office     Manager
                                                       Manager

                              Body Shop   Quality     Mechanical and
                              Foreman     Controller  Electrical Foreman
                                 |           |              |
                              Charge-hands  Testers    Charge-hands
```

but tends to be somewhat coarse in action. It requires very little attention apart from an annual check of its oil level. To William this manufacturer's gearbox compares unfavourably with others, particularly one made by a rival firm. The rival gearbox is noted for its versatility and extraordinary smoothness of operation. It is very reliable but requires adjustment about every 15,000 miles of normal wear to maintain its performance at concert pitch.

Automobiles PLC do not normally permit customers to enter the workshops. They have a well-organized reception office and require the receptionists, supported by a team of testers, to liaise between the mechanics and the Workshop Manager and the customer. However, William – who feels, probably correctly, that he is better informed than either the receptionists or the Workshop Manager on the subject of automatic transmissions – has formed a habit of coming out of the workshop to talk to the customer whenever any technical issues arise. This behaviour has been tolerated good-humouredly by the reception office staff, who accept William's expertise. The Workshop Manager, equally dependent on William's skills, has turned a blind eye to his actions.

On several occasions William has remarked to a customer

dissatisfied with the incurable coarseness and simplicity of the gearbox provided in the cars the firm distributes that, really, if refinement and versatility are required, the rival manufacturer's gearboxes are much better. He says this in a clinical and dispassionate manner, using the names of the gearboxes, not the names of the cars. Recently a customer has quoted William's observations to one of the sales staff as a reason for delaying a decision about buying a new car.

The news has reached the Sales Director and a furious row has broken out between him and the Service Director, a highly educated and trained man whose supportive loyalty to his staff is both admired and sometimes feared. Relations between the directors become so bad that the Managing Director is involved.

At the beginning of the dispute the Sales Director proposes that William be dismissed immediately. The Service Director consults the workshop senior staff and rejects this suggestion outright. William, he claims, is a very valued member of the team. Since the company undertakes servicing for many different makes of vehicle, it is essential that a senior mechanic is available whose knowledge of automatic gearboxes is much wider than that of people trained on only one type of gearbox. He admits that William's technical enthusiasm may have been indiscreet on this occasion, but points out that customers find his 'personal service' and his informed discussions extremely valuable, to such an extent that a deliberate policy of ignoring his breaches of normal protocol has developed.

The Service Director then proposes that William be warned about his conduct and told that he must not imply inferiority in the new cars the company is trying to sell. This does not satisfy the Sales Director, who now claims to have discovered other incidents in which William has prejudiced adversely the attitude of a potential customer for a new vehicle.

The Managing Director is a salesman at heart, having risen from the position of Sales Director some years ago. He finds the detached view taken by the service staff extremely irritating and this incident a further proof of a suspected disloyalty to the company's chosen manufacturer and its products.

The company has a small branch workshop about six miles away, in the district where it first began operating. The workshop has been kept going in order to maintain brand loyalty in the area, particularly as Automobiles PLC fear that customers may be seduced by the proximity of a large distributor of a rival manufacturer's cars. Most of the work done at this branch workshop is of the simpler kind. Major problems are often referred to the main workshop, with cars being ferried to and fro by the firm's drivers or on a transporter. Automatic gearbox overhauls are always done at the main workshop.

The Managing Director instructs that William be transferred as charge-hand to this out-station and the existing charge-hand, a young man, transferred to the main workshop 'to gain experience', as the MD puts it. To the Service Director's protest that his most accomplished expert will be lost to the automatic-gearbox team, the MD tartly retorts that if there is no one on the team capable of taking over from William, the Service Director has only himself to thank.

William receives a letter about this transfer from the MD but is not seen by him. In fact, William has not been consulted at all during the row and the news of the MD's decision comes as a painful shock. With the Service Director's permission, William visits the small workshop and speaks to the charge-hand, whose frank and innocent comment is, '. . . it's all oil changes and fitting new components like water pumps, changing fan belts – things like that; not your kind of high tech stuff, mate!' What is more, with some cynical amusement, the young charge-hand indicates his team of young men, most of them still in training – '. . . not like your white-coated specialists, I'm afraid!'

William is highly displeased. He believes that his skills will find a ready market elsewhere, but decides initially to act as instructed. After a month's work, during which he keeps a careful record of the class of work done, he resigns, stating in his letter that he has been demoted to an inferior position without proper cause.

William's wife is in a well-paid job at middle-management level with the local authority and the family can survive financially (all the children are self-supporting). No suitable job is currently available in the area, though William is aware that in about six months he may well be appointed to an equivalent job in a rival firm. Meanwhile, however, William takes advice and lets it be known that he will be taking his case to an industrial tribunal on the grounds that he has been constructively dismissed.

Your role in all this is that of Company Secretary. Although you have heard rumours of a considerable dispute, nothing has come to you officially and your own superior, the Financial and Administrative Director, has always been rather aloof from the bickerings between sales and service, not uncommon in the motor trade. Suddenly, however, you are requested 'as our legal adviser' to guide the MD, to give your opinion on the situation and to offer advice that will avoid future problems of this kind. You are somewhat handicapped by the fact that you have come quite recently from an organization in which all personnel issues have been handled by specialists, leaving the Company Secretary and his staff to concentrate on the accounting, costing and related issues.

Reference section

As far as the present situation is concerned, you need to make yourself familiar with the Unfair Dismissal Provisions of the Employment Protection (Consolidation) Act 1978 as amended by the Employment Acts of 1980 and 1982 as well as the ACAS Code of Practice. It will help to read *Fair and Unfair Dismissal*, which explains constructive dismissal thus:

> A tribunal may rule that an employee who resigns because of conduct by his or her employer has been 'constructively dismissed'. For a tribunal to rule in this way the employer's action has to be such that it can be regarded as a substantial breach of the employment contract indicating that he or she intends no longer to be bound by the contract: an example of this might be where the employer arbitrarily demotes an employee to a lower rank or poorer paid position. The contract is what has been agreed between the parties, whether orally or in writing or a combination of both, together with what must be necessarily implied to make the contract workable.

If the case is heard by an industrial tribunal, a great deal will depend on the view taken of William's transfer. His case is that he has been demoted to a position held by a younger and less experienced man and dealing with simple routine operations; that he has been deprived of the highly specialized work for which he is qualified and experienced; and, therefore, that he has also been deprived of possible career opportunities in the future. He will point out that the remuneration of the man he replaced was less than his, so that not only the lower level of work but also the lower level of payment indicates that he has been demoted. He will argue that he merely answered a customer's technical question and that although his answer could be embarrassing to the sales staff, he could not tell a lie.

The tribunal will need to decide whether there has been a demotion and if so, whether it is arbitrary and unjustified, or justified by William's actions.

You also need to discover what William's contract says about location. Does it demand that he works anywhere except at the main premises? Has the company, in fact, ever given all employees written notice of the main terms of their contracts and details of grievance and disciplinary procedures, as required by law (see *Written Statement of Main Terms and Conditions of Employment*)?

If the changes in William's job and location were unjustified and arbitrary, then your company may be considered to be in a substantial breach of the Employment Acts. You may wish to advise the company to come to terms with William either by reinstatement, if possible or desirable, or by financial compensation.

With regard to the future, you need to consider and give advice on the delicate matter of the Managing Director's method of dealing with the conflict. On this occasion (as apparently in the past) the MD has tried to resolve the matter by making a decision without involving middle management or seeing the central figure, William. The company has become too large and complicated for the MD's style to be other than dangerous, as legislation exists to protect employees against arbitrary decisions.

You may wish to suggest, for example, setting up a system of personnel management that requires all disciplinary problems to be considered by a works committee including middle-management and shop-floor representatives, and recommend that your director be made specifically responsible for all personnel matters. You may also wish to point out that if you are, as the MD said, 'our legal adviser', you should have been consulted in advance of the decision.

12 Weatherwear Ltd

'You're a thief!'

Weatherwear makes anoraks and similar garments. There are thirty workers, all women, engaged in making up the garments. Training is provided on the job by the forewoman, Dorothy, and her two charge-hands. They are under considerable pressure to maintain output, but the wage difference between them and the other workers is small. The other personnel are a van driver, a storeman/porter, a small office staff, two salesmen and a works manager, all presided over by the owner of the business, Ian.

The presence of such a high proportion of women would argue that maternity and associated leave would be commonplace, but in practice the low wages paid and the poor working conditions have resulted in a high turnover of personnel so that few have acquired the qualifying two years of continuous employment for at least sixteen hours per week. Conditions within the workshop are not improved by Ian's unwillingness to admit that the economic power and unrestrained control of management over employees has changed since the business was founded by his grandfather in 1920.

Relationships amongst the machinists have become strained lately because of accusations that the Works Manager, Jeffrey, who is Ian's nephew, has shown favouritism to some workers. The accusations include the suggestion that he is having an affair with Ravinder, a machinist of three years' service, and that she is being given numerous privileges, including absence from the actual production of garments. This, in particular, annoys Dorothy and her colleagues, as Ian maintains a constant watch on output, which he claims is falling.

While relations between uncle and nephew are becoming less cordial, Ian is increasing his reliance on Dorothy. Eventually he begins to control factory affairs by giving instructions directly to her, bypassing Jeffrey. In consequence of this Jeffrey decides to go into partnership with two of his friends in a nearby town, leaving Ian without a works manager and in danger of a possible loss of business.

About this time Ravinder reveals to her friends that she is pregnant. She produces a medical certificate and a clinic appointment card and requests time off with pay to attend an antenatal clinic.

The time off is grudgingly given, but when the next payday arrives it has been deducted from her wages. Recently Ravinder has read a number of articles in the local press about the alleged exploitation of clothing trade workers, especially, it is stated, those who are immigrants and have a poor grasp of the English language. She is an Asian, separated from her family and living by herself in what could be real poverty; indeed, the fact that she is not in greater financial difficulty is considered to point to the truth of the story about her relationship with Jeffrey. It is not surprising, therefore, that Ravinder seeks out the journalist who has written the articles and offers to provide information about the state of affairs at the works.

At this point another problem arises. The Chief Clerk reports that petty cash kept in a drawer in the office is being stolen. The sums are small but the losses are persistent. The police are informed and after much hesitation the local beat officer agrees to provide the means of detecting an internal thief. This attempt is entirely unsuccessful but the thefts cease.

As these events are occurring the reporter and photographer from the local paper appear at the works and seek an interview with Ian. They reveal information that could have come only from an internal source. Ian refuses to see them, so they content themselves with taking photographs and seeking former employees to interview.

Ian is in a high state of agitation when Dorothy informs him that Ravinder is demanding to be paid for her period of attendance at the antenatal clinic. It suddenly occurs to him that the press informant is not his estranged nephew, but the girl with whom he has, it is believed, been having an affair. Summoning Dorothy, who is now acting as Works Manager, Ian demands that Ravinder be dismissed.

'On what grounds?' Dorothy asks, to which Ian replies, 'Surely you can find some good reason.'

Ravinder's sharp tongue and favourite's role have left her with many enemies, particularly Dorothy, who now finds Ian's suggestion is perfectly acceptable, although not easy to act on. However, by a strange coincidence, while doing some cleaning at home Dorothy finds an old sheet of a local newspaper used to line a drawer. Glancing at a column of Magistrates' Court cases, she is surprised to see that one of them refers to Ravinder. It records that she had been found guilty of shoplifting, had admitted previous offences and been fined. This event occurred some seven years ago.

The next day Dorothy takes Ravinder into an office and tells her that her pregnancy is preventing her from carrying out her work and she should give up her job. Ravinder disagrees indignantly. She points out that her pregnancy is very little advanced and in no way affects her power to work. 'Indeed,' she says, 'the only effect is that I need to attend the antenatal clinic, for which you've deducted time, and that's wrong!'

At this point Dorothy produces what she thinks is her trump card. 'Look,' she says, 'I've tried to get you out tactfully. You could use pregnancy as an explanation and no one would know.'

'Know what?' cries Ravinder. 'What should they know?'

'Why, that you're a thief,' Dorothy replies. 'You've been convicted before and now you've started to steal here. Well, what can we expect from someone who won't even say who the father of her child is? I can't understand how you can stay – it's all over the shop.'

'If it is, it's because you've told everyone. Tell me, am I sacked?'

'Yes, you certainly are.'

'Then put it in writing.'

'I don't need to. Here's your P45, now go!'

This dialogue, heard by others through the partition, ends in Ravinder running off in tears. She does not return and Ian receives the news with satisfaction on his return to his office later in the day.

His satisfaction is short-lived. To his surprise he receives a 'Notice of Appearance' (Form IT3) from the local industrial tribunal office, indicating that a claim of unfair dismissal is being made against his firm. The next day Ian passes Jeffrey in the street, and the latter remarks, 'Well, you've bought it this time, and I'll see she's properly represented.'

Upset, Ian consults you, a fellow employer and a member of the local Chamber of Trade and Industry, and pours out what is in fact an accurate story of the events, including a verbatim account of the

Weatherwear Ltd

dialogue between Ravinder and Dorothy as conveyed to him by one of the office staff.

Reference section

The prime causes of Ian's troubles are a belief that the natural relationship between employer and hourly-paid employees is 'warfare', and a complete ignorance of modern labour legislation. To advise him properly you will need to try to deal with his attitude and provide him with basic information about the law. In particular, he needs to consider what grounds Ravinder has for action before a tribunal. The most important ones are the following.

- The dismissal, without any discussion, on the grounds of maternity. Reading 'Rights of an Expectant Mother' in *Individual Rights of Employees* will show that from the very outset the failure to pay Ravinder for the time off to attend the antenatal clinic is almost certainly a breach of the law. The following paragraph from *Fair and Unfair Dismissal* makes it seem likely that Ravinder's dismissal on grounds of her pregnancy is unlawful.

  Dismissal associated with maternity
  A woman who is expecting a baby and who has worked for her employer continuously for at least one year has the right to complain of unfair dismissal if her employer dismisses her because she is pregnant, or for a reason connected with her pregnancy, unless her condition makes it impossible for her to do her job adequately, or it would be against the law for her to do that particular job while pregnant. In such cases, the employer must offer her a suitable alternative vacancy if one is available. If there is such a vacancy, but he fails to offer it to her, her dismissal will be unfair.

- If the dismissal was made on the grounds of the conviction for shoplifting, then Ian should pay particular attention to p. 25 in *Individual Rights of Employees*. Ravinder's conviction seems likely to be a 'spent conviction' and Ravinder a 'rehabilitated person'.

  However, even if this were not so, the dismissal may not be justified, as Ian will find when he reads p. 31 in

Fair and Unfair Dismissal. There seems to be no evidence that Ravinder was the person who stole the petty cash and it is clear that offences committed outside the person's employment should not be treated as *automatic* reasons for dismissal. The question is whether the offence is relevant to the employee's duties; that is, does a conviction for shoplifting make a person unfit to sew anoraks?

- Finally, there is a minor point, which perhaps indicates the firm's unreasonable style of behaviour. Ravinder has not only received no warning, but has also been refused a written statement of the reasons for her dismissal. Failure to give such a statement to Ravinder within fourteen days of her oral or written request is unlawful (see *Individual Rights of Employees*, p. 17). You might ask Ian if his employees have proper statements of the main terms and conditions of their employment as required by law, and recommend him to read the booklet of that title.

Having received the 'Notice of Appearance' from the office of the industrial tribunal, Ian has to decide what action to take. He will find that *Fair and Unfair Dismissal* explains the procedures that have been set in motion. If Ian should seek the assistance of ACAS, or if no reconciliation occurs and the tribunal finds there has been unfair dismissal, there are three main possibilities:

1. an order for reinstatement in the work from which the person was dismissed;
2. an order for re-engagement in a different job;
3. an award of compensation.

Your advice must, of course, eventually turn again to Ian's whole style of management. He needs to make a very serious reappraisal of his attitudes.

13 ReproSelect Ltd

'I'm not that bad!'

ReproSelect produces handmade furniture to customers' own requirements, which are expressed as a design by the company's design and drawing office staff, and reproduction pieces made as far as possible to designs from the books of famous furniture makers. Because of its high prices the firm must maintain the finest standards of craftsmanship.

Twelve staff are employed in the design and manufacture of furniture: the designer and his assistant, six cabinet-makers, three apprentices and one general labourer. There are three office staff, three sales representatives (two travelling and one, part-time, in the shop), and the three owner-directors, one of whom manages the firm.

Business is very brisk. The two travelling representatives have been extremely successful in extending the company's sales to various high-quality retail firms and the company has also recently opened a shop in the village where the workshop is situated. Since this village and others in the surrounding area have become popular with visitors from abroad, the sales of the reproduction furniture have doubled, especially as the local antiques dealers are charging exceedingly high prices. The association of the reproduction furniture with genuine Chippendale or Hepplewhite designs is a very useful sales device, and each purchase is accompanied by a booklet on the history of furniture and a certificate showing the origin of the design.

The shop is open from 10.30 a.m. until 5.00 p.m., six days a week. The manning is shared by the Director and a man retired from his previous job, relieved as necessary by one of the office staff and occasionally by an apprentice. The retired man and his wife have now decided to sell their house and move near their daughter and her husband in another part of the country. This will make it necessary to recruit a new member of staff, and the Director thinks that it would be sensible, at the same time to extend the shop hours to 10.00 a.m. to 5.30 p.m.

There is also a more serious personnel difficulty concerning one of the craftsmen, Alfred, who is 23 and has worked at ReproSelect for two years. Alfred was trained in the workshop of an antique restorer in a neighbouring town and is a good craftsman but no more, and certainly not up to the standard of the firm. His real interests lie in social history and the visual arts. He is, in fact, a good amateur watercolourist.

Alfred was employed at ReproSelect mainly out of respect for his father, Sam, a craftsman of extraordinary distinction, whose recent retirement has been a great loss to the firm. In fact, even now Sam's advice is sought quite frequently by the foreman, Jack, an excellent supervisor who knows his own limitations in craft skill. As a father, however, Sam had a serious failing: he could not grasp that not everyone wished to become, or was capable of becoming, a cabinet-maker of his merit. He imposed his will on his youngest son and had him apprenticed. His elder son and daughter were less biddable and have pursued different careers.

Alfred is not on very good terms with Jack, as there have been an increasing number of instances when furniture deliveries have had to be delayed because Alfred's work had to be redone by another cabinet-maker. This has resulted in the loss of time and materials, and, on one occasion, the customer's good will. To make matters worse, Alfred, who lives with his parents, is conscious of Sam's irritation as the news of events is leaked to him on his visits to the workshop. Nevertheless, Alfred does not find his situation easy to improve. He does not want to leave the village, where he is courting a local girl, and he hasn't been able to find alternative work. These pressures make him anxious and very touchy.

Matters come to a climax when Alfred and Jack have a sharp disagreement about the standard of some of Alfred's work, a standard that would be satisfactory to most firms but not to ReproSelect. Jack continues to meet Sam in the local pub and tells him frankly of the problem he has with Alfred. The old man remarks, 'You'd better sack him. He's useless at the craft – the only things he's interested in are history and painting. He'll get some other job – he'd be OK on a building site – and then perhaps he'd be away from home and learn to stand on his own feet.' Jack is surprised at the outburst, but values Sam's opinion, particularly as it confirms his own. He makes an appointment with the Director.

The Director is very preoccupied by two things. First, his wife has had to go to hospital and he is worried about her. Second, one of the representatives has brought back a splendid inquiry from an American department store. If this can be turned into a firm order, the Director can see the company's future assured for many years – perhaps until his retirement.

When Jack suggests that Alfred be dismissed for incompetence, adding that even Sam recommended such a course of action, the Director is not as displeased as Jack expected. He tells Jack that he is especially anxious about standards of workmanship, as the potential American buyers are known to have broken off a contract with another firm because they felt that standards were not being maintained. He therefore agrees that Alfred must go. His departure will coincide with one of the apprentices, a young man of enormous ability, coming out of his time, and the hiring of a youth who has obtained a grade A at A level and is renowned for the skill he has already acquired.

Alfred is called into the Director's office the following day. The Director's embarrassment makes the meeting difficult and it comes to a conclusion when he hands Alfred a letter, which states:

> Although your standard of skill is sound and equal to the demands of most business it is not good enough for us since we are renowned for the excellence of our work and can only succeed by keeping up our reputation.
>
> You are therefore given one month's notice of dismissal and we shall be pleased to assist you by providing a reference for any job suitable for you for which you apply.

The Director then tells Alfred, 'I should get off now, you'll want to go home.'

The next day the Director, having had good news of his wife, leaves for a four-week tour of America.

Alfred is hurt and worried by this unexpected dismissal. Although conscious of his lack of real love for his work, he believes that he has always been a loyal and conscientious worker of adequate, if not distinguished, skill. He knows that this is the first time he has been accused of being incompetent to do the work at the firm. An attempt to discuss this with Jack is rebuffed.

Alfred's girlfriend is very disturbed on his behalf and asks the advice of her father, a shop steward at the local brewery. He suggests that Alfred should plead unfair dismissal at an industrial tribunal and promises to help him.

Reference section

Incapacity to do the job is one of the five reasons that can justify dismissal (see *Fair and Unfair Dismissal*, p. 6), but there are many other considerations that industrial tribunals take into account.

Before an employee is dismissed for incapacity to perform his work he should first be told in what respect he is failing to do his job adequately, warned of possible dismissal and given an opportunity to improve his performance. Failure by an employer to discharge one of these responsibilities towards an employee may cause a tribunal to consider that the dismissal is unreasonable. Has Repro-Select complied with any of these obligations?

There is also some responsibility on an employer to seek to provide other work as an alternative to dismissal. The weight given to this factor will depend on the circumstances in each case. In Alfred's case there does seem to be an opportunity to avoid dismissal and assist the company. It will be recalled that the shop hours are to be extended and that a man working there is to retire. The shop sells reproduction furniture accompanied by a booklet about the history of furniture and a certificate giving the origin of the design. Alfred's interest in history and visual matters might make him a very useful shop worker, perhaps with some involvement with the design staff.

Should this case go before a tribunal, the result is not easy to foresee but the whole time-consuming business might be avoided by a serious effort at conciliation and the offer of the shop job.

14 Fabricators and Finishers Ltd

'She's anybody's!'

The atmosphere in the paint shop of this firm, which employs eighty people, has been tense for some time and this tension has now led to open violence. The two principals are Leslie and William.

Leslie is 28 and has been with the company for ten years. He is married and has two children. Leslie is a fine-looking man, but far less intelligent than he might appear on first acquaintance. His major interest is coarse fishing, which he is prepared to spend hours doing in all weathers, sometimes alone, sometimes in competitions or with a friend. His wife, Beth, a former member of the firm's office staff, now does part-time work as a 'temp'. She is a very vigorous woman and extremely attractive to most men not only because of her appearance, but also because of her capacity for flattery in pursuit of their attention.

William is the charge-hand. He is 34, and has eight years' service with the company. He was divorced some six years ago – about the time that Leslie and Beth married – and now lives with his parents.

When Beth worked at the firm much comment was caused by her frequent journeys through the factory – which were unnecessary since better routes were available – and the way in which William discovered reasons why they should visit the stores together. Suddenly, however, these activities ceased. Beth was seen to be very tearful and unhappy while, gossips were quick to notice, William was now often seen in the company of another woman, who did not work in the factory.

Before long Beth was seen keeping company with Leslie. Their engagement was soon announced and their first child was born about six months after the wedding – 'a bit premature,' claimed Beth. A second child was born two years later. Beth had always indicated that in her view women proved themselves by having children – proved themselves, she remarked, 'as women who can get what they want and do what they want'.

At present Leslie is clearly losing ground in Beth's volatile affections, and she has begun to flatter and be attentive towards one of the salesmen.

William too has suffered some disappointment, as the woman he had been going out with soon abandoned him. Since then he has been keeping company with women, but without forming a serious relationship with any of them. William is not really a very nice man. Jealous of Leslie's marriage, he begins mocking him that Beth, if not actually unfaithful, is rapidly approaching that state with not one but several men.

There have been several bitter outbursts of mocking, taunting and threatening. The mocking and taunting have come mainly from William and the threats from both. The men have been warned by Javid, the young Works Manager, who finds the situation rather beyond his control. He is currently looking for a way to separate the two men, but this is proving difficult as neither has skills other than those of the paint-shop work. Both men are competent and loss of labour in the paint shop would be a danger to production.

Recently Javid has, on the advice of his secretary, an astute middle-aged woman, been reading over the company's terms of employment, which are issued to all the staff. One item particularly interests him. It states: '(3) Any act of violence by one employee towards another will result in the immediate dismissal of the offending person.' While still trying to find means of separating the two men, whose behaviour is creating a bitter atmosphere and affecting other members of the paint shop, he is also ready and waiting for an opportunity to dismiss either one or both of them should the situation get worse or further endanger morale.

One morning a minor issue over a spray-gun develops into a violent quarrel. In the course of this William taunts Leslie with Beth's alleged infidelity, shouting, 'Anyone can have her. I used to in the stores, as everyone but you knows! Have you ever wondered about the parentage of your children?'

Leslie lifts his hand in a threatened blow but is forestalled by William, who mockingly strikes him on the face. Leslie picks up a

Fabricators and Finishers Ltd

spanner and strikes William a glancing blow. Other men fail in an attempt to part them and soon they are exchanging savage blows with their fists.

Javid is summoned and, with the aid of the yard and assembly shop foremen, two very powerful men, the combatants are dragged apart shouting obscenities and vicious threats at each other. By this time Javid is alarmed, upset and very angry. He and the two foremen escort Leslie and William to the factory gate. There Javid tells them, 'By reason of rule 3, which deals with fighting, I am dismissing you both for gross misconduct. Your P45s will be sent on to you. And don't fight outside the factory or I'll send for the police and really make trouble for you!'

Somewhat quietened, the two men go off in different directions. Beth soon hears what has been said about her and promptly directs her attention to convincing Leslie of her fidelity and her affection for him.

Poor Javid is now hoping for a less harassed life but he is disappointed. Both men claim unfair dismissal and he receives the customary 'Notice of Appearance' from an industrial tribunal. He and the Managing Director sit in the latter's office discussing the matter. 'We should have got rid of one or both of them ages ago,' remarks the Managing Director. 'And now I suppose we should ask the other men what actually happened.'

Reference section

Fighting and violence are well-established forms of misconduct for which a single offence can justify summary dismissal. In this firm that fact is indicated by the disciplinary rule quoted by Javid. Nevertheless, an industrial tribunal can take into account such matters as provocation, self-defence, the extent of the violence and other mitigating factors.

In this case Leslie has certainly received gross provocation. However, he appears to have threatened William, who may now try to argue that he was placed in fear of assault and therefore struck Leslie in self-defence.

The true cause of the fight is not something with which the employers are involved but there are some matters in which they could have improved their handling of the affair. First and foremost, they have failed to immediately obtain explanations from each man in a comparatively calm atmosphere or to take immediate statements from witnesses. They have therefore acted precipitately – which is very easy to do when faced with violence.

Second, they did not suceed in improving the earlier quarrelsome situation by, perhaps, giving stern written, rather than oral, warnings to both men that advised them on their future conduct.

How an industrial tribunal will view the men's pleas when all the facts are revealed is not easy to predict. It could be that neither man will succeed, but if either is found to have been unfairly dismissed, it is more likely to be Leslie than William.

Should the tribunal decide in their favour, their separation would have to be treated as a matter of urgency. However, harmony within the paint shop will be hard to restore if these two men are reinstated there; the departure of one or, preferably, both is the only real cure. Immediate thought needs to be given to their replacement.

15 Econclothiers Ltd

'Don't be so unfriendly, my dear!'

Phillip is the Sales Office Manager of Econclothiers, which does a large trade in cut-price clothing, normally garments of good quality that have to be sold off for one reason or another. He is a flamboyant figure, always very elaborately dressed and exuding a rakish confidence, especially in his power to charm women. In fact, his private life is not quite so satisfactory to him as the outward show of confidence would lead one to suppose. Women who have had a close personal relationship with him have expressed surprise and disappointment to their close friends. However, to most of the younger women on the staff he is either a glamorous figure or a person to be kept at arm's length.

Until recently Phillip's behaviour, though tiresome, has been largely a matter of questions and observations in bad taste. For example, he closely questioned a member of staff on whether she wore tights or stockings and suspenders, and commented at length on the erotic possibilities of these and other garments. Recently, the women in the sales office have noticed that it has become necessary to keep out of reach of his hands.

One young girl, Molly, has been found in tears because, she said, 'He tried to kiss and touch me.' This incident caused considerable anger, and one of the older women spoke to Phillip. She suggested that further such behaviour might result in 'our setting about you with the packing-room shears – that would cool you down!' Phillip took this as a tribute to his virility, but his behaviour was more controlled.

The senior management of the firm got to know of the situation but felt that it had been exaggerated and that it was 'all a bit of silly horseplay', to be discouraged but no other action taken. As one of them said to him. 'Watch it, Phil, or we'll let them do what they threatened!'

Molly, who is only 17 and rather lacking in self-confidence, leaves the company on the advice of her older sister, who, in fact, finds her a new job. Molly is replaced by 26-year-old Gwen, a neat, quietly-dressed person who, for all her demure appearance, is very resolute. Her physical beauty at once attracts Phillip's attention. He proceeds rapidly from his usual line of sexual innuendo to manual approaches, which Gwen firmly fends off. In his folly, Phillip decides she is rebuffing him in order to encourage him and, therefore, redoubles his attentions.

Gwen does not waste much time discussing Phillip and his harassment, although she lets everyone in the office know about his actions. When his behaviour becomes especially outrageous, she strikes him with a degree of skill and force that indicates that she has had some training in the art of self-defence.

Left with the clear signs of this rebuttal and, as he correctly feels, the object of contempt and mockery from most of his female colleagues, Phillip is determined not to endure his shameful and public defeat without an attempt at revenge. The opportunity is not long in coming.

The firm has a strict rule that all transactions should be entered in the computer cash and stock record system. On this occasion Gwen had received a number of cheques and notes, but before she had time to enter them she was summoned to the reception office. Before going she slipped the cheques and notes into a drawer. At reception she was told by a police officer that her car had been found stolen and vandalized, and that he would drive her to it. Hastily leaving a message in reception, she went with the police officer.

No sooner had Gwen gone than a customer telephoned to say that he thought he might have dated his cheque incorrectly and could this be checked. A search by Phillip eventually resulted in the cheque being discovered in the drawer. This treatment of money was in total contradiction of the company's rules in the written contract: '. . . all monies received must be recorded in the computerized cash and stock record and failure to carry out this rule shall be regarded as cause for immediate dismissal.'

Phillip goes at once to the company Financial Director and is given permission to discharge Gwen forthwith. On her return to the office she is given her letter of dismissal. Gwen immediately begins proceedings before an industrial tribunal, claiming unfair dismissal on the grounds that one act of inadvertence, which would have been corrected immediately she returned, is not of itself sufficient reason, despite the company's rule, to justify instant dismissal. She also gets in touch with Molly, having heard the reason for her departure.

To add to the problems of the company, which depends for its reputation on the swift and efficient handling of orders, the sales office staff now threaten to refuse to work with Phillip and demand his dismissal. Two of the older women, whose expertise is particularly valuable, have already found other jobs and hand in their notice, giving their dislike of Phillip's conduct as a reason.

Reference section

This situation arises entirely from the failure of the management to halt sexual harassment of female employees by a member of the middle management.

An industrial tribunal would give serious consideration to Gwen's plea that a single, honest mistake in the stress of the moment could not be regarded as an intentional action or a persistent failure of duty sufficient to warrant dismissal. The ACAS Code of Practice makes this clear and *Fair and Unfair Dismissal* points out that the reason for dismissal must be not only valid but also reasonable in the particular circumstances. It also explains that the employee's explanation must be heard and taken into consideration.

Molly, if she chooses, could probably argue that her own departure amounted to constructive dismissal because of persistent sexual harassment. If Gwen and Molly do not have the service (two years) to enable them to claim unfair dismissal, they could do equally well by claiming sex discrimination, for which there is no qualifying period. The fact that the employer knew of Phillip's activities and took no decisive action to stop them suggests that Molly and Gwen would win their claim – and this is especially true in Gwen's case.

The moral of the story is that, as management have discovered many times, social problems, of which sexual harassment is one especially serious example, inevitably lead to generalized problems, frequently involving the loss of morale, unwelcome resignations and undesirable publicity.

16 The Component Co. Ltd

'It was for the baby, not me!'

You are the proprietor of this small manufacturing company. You have other small companies and your home is the management HQ for all of them. You are faced with the following circumstances.

Maureen, who is 18, is the mother of a small baby. The child's father has left her and disappeared. Maureen's parents are dead and she has no close relatives, so she relies on an elderly woman, to whom she pays a small sum, to care for the child while she goes to work.

The company operates in an extremely competitive market and Maureen's work is not well paid. Her wages consist of a very low basic rate of £55 per week net, to which a piece-work system adds another £10. She lives in a privately rented flat, consisting of a bed-sitting-room, kitchen and bathroom, for which she pays £35 per week. This leaves her with £30 a week plus her child allowance to pay all domestic expenses. During the winter, in particular, she has great difficulty in making ends meet.

Maureen is not an intelligent girl and has no idea of any legitimate way of increasing her income. She occasionally lets her thoughts wander towards some not necessarily legal action that will increase her resources. She has already stolen odd items of baby food and managed to walk away with far more than she paid for at a jumble sale.

Her work consists of using a small, relatively simple machine to produce a metal component. By improving one's dexterity it is possible to speed up the various operations and so produce more components and earn more piece-work bonus. The components are collected by a labourer, weighed in the finished-goods store, and the output recorded for the purpose of wage calculations. This is the only check, as the machine itself does not record its output.

The Component Co. Ltd

The person who weighs the components is a dour and gloomy woman, who dislikes young people in general and unmarried mothers in particular. The labourer, on the other hand, is a kind, good-natured young man two years older than Maureen. Like Maureen, Tommy is far from intelligent, and he is not well informed.

Maureen is herself a kind, open-hearted girl and despite her troubles seems to maintain her sense of fun. This apparent cheerfulness is superficial, however. One day Tommy finds her alone in the workshop in tears and she tells him all about her financial difficulties. Carefully checking to see that the stores are empty, he goes in and returns a few of the components that Maureen has made to her half-filled tray. Thus these are checked twice and credited twice. This practice continues and Maureen's piece-work bonus is increased from £10 a week to about £12.50.

After several weeks the checker becomes suspicious. Covertly observing Maureen, she comes to the conclusion that the girl's rate of working remains as it always was. She suggests to the Foreman that Maureen's output is too good to be true. A watch is kept and the two young people are caught.

The discovery produces a small crisis in the management team. The Works Manager, Foreman, Office Manager and the Stores Manager meet to discuss the situation. The following suggestions are made:

- Dismiss Maureen for dishonesty and inform the police that by this means she has stolen £10 approximately.

- Dismiss Maureen for dishonesty.

- Warn Maureen and give her a different job.

- Dismiss Tommy for aiding Maureen in dishonesty, and inform the police.

- Dismiss Tommy for dishonesty.

- Warn Tommy and give him a different job.

While these arguments are in progress one of the other workshop personnel insists on being heard by the management and tells them the facts about Maureen's situation. This produces a mixture of reactions ranging from generalized denunciations of modern wickedness to compassion.

To avoid any immediate decision it is suggested that both young people be interviewed again. Tommy is found, much distressed, but Maureen has disappeared. One of the van drivers puts his head round the door to say he has seen her standing on the road to the motorway with a baby and a suitcase trying to get a lift.

At this point the Works Manager and his secretary go to try to stop Maureen from leaving the area. They succeed and take her home. The secretary offers to stay with her for a while and the Works Manager returns to the factory. He telephones you at your home and asks you for your decision.

Reference section

All decisions have an ethical context even though it may be concealed beneath a mass of legal and other considerations. Here the question, which cannot ever be totally evaded, is to what extent are employers responsible for the welfare of an employee other than in respect of justice within the operations of the organization as defined by law and in regard to health and safety. In other words, are Maureen's problems any concern of the company?

Maureen and Tommy have committed clear acts of deliberate dishonesty. However, neither has been guilty of such an offence towards the company before. Industrial tribunals regard dishonesty as a serious offence and probably Maureen and Tommy could be dismissed without fear of decision against the company. Whether the police would wish them to be prosecuted is another matter; if they did, they might recommend that both be placed under the supervision of a probation officer.

It is this possibility that leads to consideration of the company's responsibility in ethical terms. If such a responsibility is accepted, then an analysis of the situation reveals that the root cause of Maureen's problem is the lack of any advice and counselling that would have enabled her to overcome her financial problems. As for Tommy, his impulsive conduct has, in fact, been the cause of Maureen's dishonesty since he initiated the scheme, although he gained nothing from it.

The Component Co. Ltd

Any solution to this problem must take into consideration the future of two rather silly young people and one baby. It must also accept the fact that other workers in the factory may have distinctly uncompromising and suspicious views about Maureen and Tommy hereafter. Moreover, it is necessary to avoid appearing to be actually rewarding two dishonest people or suggesting that all employees are allowed one dishonest act. Three issues are especially important:

1. Maureen's financial problems must be solved, which can be done with the aid of the appropriate agencies.
2. Tommy's folly must be made clear to him, although to dismiss him could condemn him to prolonged unemployment.
3. If Maureen and Tommy remain, they must be separated when at work.

You may wish to consider why in this small company so little is known of individual problems and needs and whether someone should be made responsible for staff welfare.

17 Finishing Productions PLC

'Look! They've got holes in them'

Selwyn, Khan and Liam work in the pickling shop at Finishing Productions. Their work consists in the immersion of ferrous materials, such as fabricated parts, tubes and rods, in hot acidic baths to prepare them for the application of protective coatings. The process involves several immersions in acid. As the goods treated are not alike nor in large batches, the cages containing the materials to be treated are lowered into the tanks using hand-controlled hoists. There is a great deal of acid about, the floors are wet and slippery, and from time to time more acid is added from carboys to maintain the acidic strength of the pickle.

It is an old-fashioned, rather crude process, but cheap and effective. It depends on the willingness of the three men concerned to endure unpleasant conditions and because of those conditions the turnover of labour is considerable. In fact, only one man has stuck to the job for more than a year, most of them staying for no more than a few months.

The longest-serving worker is Selwyn, who has been employed for thirty months. Khan and Liam have been employed for only three and two months respectively. Selwyn's main reason for staying on is that he has five children and has discouraged his wife from working to increase the family income.

The main terms and conditions of employment provided by the firm state: '. . . employees engaged in any process involving any hazard are required to wear the correct protective apparatus, appliances, clothing and boots as supplied by the company. Failure to do so may result in summary dismissal.' In addition, in the pickling shop the following notice, much defaced but still legible, is stuck to the wall:

Finishing Productions PLC

> *Protective equipment – Pickling Shop*
> Long rubber gloves
> Rubber boots (Wellington type)
> Rubber aprons
> The above are to be worn at all times by employees engaged in pickling operations.

Some eighteen months ago the company was taken over by another organization of similar size – that is, fifty workshop employees. It is frequently stated in gossip that Finishing Productions will be closed down eventually in order to concentrate all work at the new owner's plant and release this very valuable site for sale. Certainly the state of the equipment seems to bear this out, as there is a general tendency to patch up rather than replace. The management are either young and looking forward to finding other work or being transferred, or are older and fearing unemployment should they lose their present jobs.

For some time Selwyn, who by length of service has become a kind of leading hand, has been pointing out that the protective clothing is not protective. As a result of age and use the rubber gloves have holes in them at the fingers, the boots have very smooth soles and allow the wearers to slip, and the aprons have tears and holes.

Khan and Liam are already contemplating leaving for other jobs if they can find them or, in Khan's case, to work in a family business. Even unemployment would seem better than enduring the general conditions in the pickling shop, where fumes from galvanizing baths are also polluting the atmosphere.

Selwyn's complaints meet with little response. The Galvanizing Foreman, who is responsible for the pickling shop, fears redundancy and is very anxious to do nothing that will attract unfavourable attention. However, he is only 35 and his fears are nothing compared to those of the Works Manager, who is 58, completely unqualified and by no means likely to obtain further employment should he lose his job.

Both of the men have become acutely sensitive to the new employer's reluctance to spend much money. This attitude was made evident when the failure of a fan that forced galvanizing fumes into a ventilating stack was dealt with only when the brewery owning a neighbouring pub complained that the fumes were rolling across the street into the saloon bar. Therefore they make only a very casual mention of Selwyn's complaints to the new management. The hints about the need to replace the protective clothing, while protecting themselves, were easily ignored.

One evening Selwyn returns home with acid 'burns' on his fingers and holes in his trousers and his underwear. His wife is most distressed and consults her father, an operating-theatre technician, and her mother, who is a midwife. Both are indignant and Selwyn's father-in-law consults his union shop steward. As a result he gives Selwyn some advice and helps him draft the following letter to the Works Manager:

> Dear Sir
> I have repeatedly asked for replacement of the worn-out protective clothing in the pickling shop but this has not been done.
>
> My terms of employment say that employees must wear the protective clothing listed in our shop. It is useless and because of this I have been injured by acid and my clothes damaged.
>
> I think you have broken your contract unless you replace the clothing at once.
>
> Yours faithfully,
> Selwyn

There is no written response to Selwyn's letter, but he has an angry conversation with the Works Manager in the presence of Liam and Khan. The Works Manager's final sentence sums it up: 'They'll have to do for the time being; the works is going to be closed before long. If you don't want to work here you can go. There's plenty who'll be glad of the job. After all, your money's good – you can't deny that.'

Selwyn cannot deny that. Nevertheless, after waiting for a fortnight for some practical response by way of new protective clothing, he leaves the job without notice. He has been encouraged to do so by his wife, who says that she would rather be poor than have him injured. Shortly afterwards Finishing Productions Ltd receive a 'Notice of Appearance' from the office of the local industrial tribunal.

Finishing Productions PLC

Selwyn has complained that he has been forced to leave because of his employer's breach of contract, resulting in his unfair dismissal.

On realizing that Selwyn has left for good, Liam and Kahn each give one week's notice and leave on its expiry.

Reference section

The safety of employees involves both moral and legal obligations. This is a case of constructive dismissal (see p. 74), so the question is, first, whether the employer has dismissed the employee. In other words, has the employer indicated by his actions and behaviour that he no longer intends to be bound by the contract of employment by being guilty of a breach of an implied term of the contract. If so, then the employee has been dismissed. The next point is to ask: what is the employer's reason for the dismissal. If he denies dismissal then he cannot easily give a reason! If he does try to show a reason, the tribunal will be hard to satisfy.

The company has issued written terms of employment that state that failure to wear the protective clothing provided could lead to summary dismissal. In fact, the protective clothing provided is said to be useless. Irrespective of any breaches of safety legislation, which would need separate examination, it would seem that a tribunal could regard Selwyn as having been unfairly constructively dismissed, entitled to leave without notice and eligible for compensation. Liam and Khan, of course, have not been employed for long enough to be eligible for compensation.

The management need to read the passages on dismissal in *Fair and Unfair Dismissal* (pp. 6–7, 17) and *Individual Rights of Employees* (pp. 17–20).

Quite apart from the legal implications of what has happened, the story points a moral about communication within an organization. Poor morale usually leads to poor patterns of communication, just as much as poor communication leads to poor morale.

Although the new employer has been very reluctant to spent large sums of money on new fixed equipment, there is probably less reason to suppose that he would have rejected minor expenditure on new protective clothing, which, unlike the fan, could eventually have been added to the stock of the main works, had the case been put clearly and firmly and not by fear-ridden hints. Had the two managers involved been clear about the future and been given proper instructions about the way in which the business was to be conducted for the time being, the whole affair would not have taken place. Indeed, the company is fortunate that the failure to provide proper protective clothing has not led to serious injury and really costly problems.

The immediate effect will be a decrease in production, as in the short term men will have to be moved from other work to pickling while new staff is found and trained. The men who are moved from other work will probably insist on proper protective clothing.

18 Anticorro PLC

'No one's been that fussy before!'

Anticorro PLC is a small firm that provides a range of products that protect plant and equipment from acid liquids and fumes and can be used to convey such liquids and fumes. One of its most important products is a powder that is converted to a thick material by heating in a cast-iron pot. While extremely hot, it is spread on the area to be protected, using plasterers' trowels and 'floats'; often tiles are set in it and joints pointed with it.

This product is supplied to customers in its powder form or is converted and conveyed to the site in heated buckets and applied by workmen employed by Anticorro. The unmelted powder is carcinogenic if inhaled over a period of years. To what extent the fumes from the heated pot are dangerous is not clearly established.

Down the years there have been frequent major and minor instances in which employees have been burned by the hot material, which, because of its treacle-like consistency, is hard to remove once it has alighted on the skin. The burns usually leave scars, and long-service employees can be distinguished from newcomers by the scars on their hands and arms and, occasionally, on their legs.

The company has a Safety Code, which defines the protective clothing to be used and the circumstances in which it is to be worn. The main points in the Code, which are designed to deal with the danger of both dust inhalation and burns, are shown below.

1. Protective clothing and masks supplied
   a. Dust masks with renewable filter elements
   b. Gauntlet gloves
   c. Foundryman's leggings
   d. Strong boots with steel toecaps
2. Application

a. Persons employed in melting and preparing material will wear masks, gauntlet gloves, leggings and strong boots.
b. Persons employed in taking the material from the melting pot to those applying it will wear gauntlet gloves, leggings and strong boots.
c. Persons employed in applying the material will wear gauntlet gloves, leggings and strong boots.

Rule 2a is generally observed except that the usual practice is for masks to be worn when handling sacks of powder and emptying them into the pot but not while supervising the melting. Rule 2b is partially observed: gloves and strong boots are usually worn but leggings less consistently. Rule 2c is also partially observed: the places in which the work is carried out are often hot – for example, in a metal-melting shop – so that the gloves and leggings become oppressive and are removed. Craftsmen also sometimes remove their gauntlet gloves because they are too clumsy when, for example, setting tiles in awkward situations.

Another problem is that the protective gear is frequently lost or damaged as the small gangs move to and from the depot and various sites. Damage or loss at work sites perhaps a hundred or more miles from the depot often results in a period of working without the necessary equipment. In theory a foreman who is faced with stopping work until replacement equipment arrives can buy it locally out of his own pocket with the promise of reimbursement. There are inevitably delays in reimbursement and arguments over failure to produce receipts.

Various methods of ensuring that safety equipment is used have been tried. At one time allowances were made to regular employees to buy their own equipment, which they were supposed to carry with them. This failed to work because casual and new labour were not adequately provided for, while some men failed to use the allowance correctly and arguments arose over requests for money to replace equipment lost – 'carelessly', to quote the Cashier.

Another idea the company tried was for customers to provide equipment, with an allowance made against the contract price. This resulted in arguments on site when the equipment was not available or was incorrect.

The present system is for the Construction Manager's clerk to complete an equipment schedule for each and every job, which authorizes the stores to load up on the transport the correct equipment. Losses are considerable and a frequent source of irritation.

Thus, in practice, safety precautions vary in their efficiency from gang to gang and job to job, with an obvious tendency to pay them merely lip service. In fact, men can be observed ritually putting on equipment when members of the HQ staff are seen to be arriving. Excuses for non-usage are plentiful and often repeated: 'I've only taken them off to wipe the sweat off my hands', 'This mask doesn't seem to let me breathe properly', 'I'm off to the toilet so I've taken off my gloves', and so on.

Very recently the senior management have turned from the weary acceptance of an inefficient and frequently neglected system towards rigorous imposition of precautions at all jobs. The reasons for this change in attitude were two successful legal actions against the company by:

- the widow of a man whose death from cancer was attributed medically to the inhalation of the dry powder over the fifteen years he was a melter;

- by the dependants of an employee who suffered burns on his arm, which became infected and resulted in his death.

In the first case the claimant was able to produce evidence that masks were often defective or were not available at all times. In the other case the claimant produced evidence that for the work being done at the time of the burn the only equipment available was of such a nature as would have rendered successful execution of the work virtually impossible.

In both cases the court heard that supervisory staff turned a blind eye to breaches of the company's Safety Code and that they were encouraged to do so by the various organizational problems that were common. The court awarded substantial damages and costs to both claimants.

The Managing Director, who has only recently taken charge of the firm, has had a great deal of experience of dangerous processes. In setting reforms in progress, he has conducted various surveys, which have revealed great inefficiency in stores management and loss of materials either by dishonesty or, more probably, by negligence. Amongst the matters with which he has been concerned has been the frequent abandonment on site of much portable material and equipment. He now insists that foremen must account for all failures to return equipment and unused material to the depot. This reform is not very popular since it entails far more careful supervision and accurate communication than before.

In addition to cutting out waste, the new MD is determined that there shall be no fatalistic acceptances of perils and that safety precautions shall be strongly enforced. He is a humane but highly paternalistic individual whose style of management can be distinctly autocratic. Middle management of his own choosing usually like and respect him, but some of the longer serving men find him interfering and oppressive. In particular, they resent his determination to tighten up site practice. His own view of safety is summarized by a remark he made soon after his arrival. 'If people insist on inhaling noxious powder or burning themselves when at home I can't stop them, but no one shall ever say that negligence or lack of discipline on my part has ever killed anyone on one of our jobs!

A notice is issued to all supervisory staff that 'failure to carry out the company's Code of Safe Practice at all times shall be treated as grounds for dismissal.' A similar warning is given to all other personnel and to all casual staff on engagement. At a meeting with middle-managers and foremen the MD explains his policy and makes it clear that he expects it to be carried out.

For some weeks all goes well. Then one day a newly appointed travelling supervisor on the Construction Manager's staff visits a site some distance from the depot. When he arrives at 2.15 p.m., he discovers the melter, Ralph, pouring powder into the melting pot without a mask, leggings or gloves. The supervisor, Mark, asks Ralph for an explanation of what he describes as 'a flagrant, deliberate and dangerous breach of safety precautions'. Ralph explains that the mask filter is not working properly, the leggings are too hot and the gloves are not necessary at this point.

An examination of the mask does indicate that a new filter is

Anticorro PLC

needed and in fact a pack of these was included in the site delivery schedule. At this point the foreman, Tom, who has been in consultation with his customer's Works Manager in the customer's offices half a mile away, returns to the site. He explains that the pack of filters is in the boot of his car. 'I have them there for safety, but people have only to ask!' A row involving all three men begins.

Ralph, 60, is unqualified and has risen from labouring to his semi-skilled position. He is not really very intelligent but once he has grasped something it sticks. He has been continuously employed by the firm for ten years and before that as a casual worker. He is a bachelor and lives with his widowed sister.

Tom is 35 and joined the company five years ago. He was once a plasterer but found this work more interesting. Separated from his wife and children, he also feels happier when travelling from place to place.

Mark is 45. He was previously a skilled tiler and then a foreman. He has worked for the company for nine years.

Ralph is quite good at his job but has no ambition. He just wants to carry on as before and is determined not to overwork. Tom and Mark are ambitious. Mark wants to be Construction Manager when the present incumbent, currently on holiday, leaves. Tom wants Mark's job. They both see that their futures must involve pleasing their new MD

Ralph has a considerable capacity for drink and usually considers four pints of beer at midday a reasonable allowance before the afternoon's work. Provided he's not crossed, he is, drunk or sober, the soul of affability. However, when he feels he is being patronized or bullied, he turns surly and then aggressive. He is of Irish extraction and proud of that country's history. He was a soldier and loves to boast of the way 'the Irish have fought England's wars'.

The conversation on safety goes wrong from the start when Mark observes, 'You drunken Paddys are all alike – lovely lads if it weren't for the drink and this bloody careless style; no regard for a simple instruction.' In a few moments threats are being uttered and shortly afterwards Ralph has been dismissed for refusal to carry out a written instruction on safety and gross misconduct in threatening Mark and Tom. Restrained by his mates from attacking the other two men, Ralph leaves the site and returns to his lodgings without having put forward any further justification of his actions. Later that evening a very drunken Ralph is placed on a train home by his mates.

Ralph's sister is a resolute and protective woman. On understanding the situation, made clearer by a conversation with the wife of one of the gang, she goes to the Citizens' Advice Bureau, where she is given details about industrial tribunals. Soon after that the company is told that Ralph is claiming to have been unfairly dismissed. The MD is not pleased and the Construction Manager is greeted on return from his holiday with a brusque demand for an explanation and a solution.

It could well be that the fact that the 'new safety policy' has been properly communicated to all personnel would be sufficient for the tribunal to find in favour of the company. However, it could be that conciliation would be a wiser policy, especially in view of Ralph's long association with Anticorro PLC.

Reference section

This is an example of the way in which a basically sound policy can be wrecked by a failure to communicate and hasty actions. The points at issue are whether there is a valid reason for dismissing the employee and whether the employer is acting reasonably in treating that reason as sufficient for dismissal (see *Fair and Unfair Dismissal*, pp. 6, 8–10).

In this instance the Construction Manager may ask himself:

- Does the employee really understand that the new rules differ from the past in their 'absoluteness'?
- Is the offence such as to justify summary dismissal?
- Has the employee been able to put his point of view?

The fact is that Ralph can argue that he has been unfairly dismissed because breaches of the company's Safety Code have been not only frequent but condoned by the management. The MD's new policy has to be carried out by employees, but there is nothing in Ralph's record to show that he has been in any way especially defiant in respect of safety regulations; this was the first time he had been accused of a breach of the Safety Code. His explanation about the filter in the mask was a statement of fact and his explanation about leggings and gloves were excuses often used and accepted from the past. His conduct was simply a belated example of a general practice. The fact that he smelled of drink and made aggressive threats does not help him but the supervisor's ill-timed remarks about 'Paddys' might be regarded as provocative.

An attempt at conciliation seems desirable. There is also much to be said for putting the problems of safety to the men, other than managers and supervisors, at one or more meetings rather than by issuing threatening notices, which may well be seen merely as a management effort 'to cover' itself.

19 L & L Ltd

'The compulsory take-away'

L & L Ltd makes adults' and children's garments. The twelve making-up machinists, all women, receive the sum of £1.40 an hour, which in a normal week gives a wage of £56.

Oscar, the owner of the business, runs a restaurant next door. On recruitment, these workers are informed that they are required to take their lunch, at the cost of £1.20 a day, from the take-away department of the restaurant. Because of complaints about having to have a meal each day, Oscar has issued vouchers that can be saved and used at any time, including the evenings and weekends. The vouchers are put in each pay packet with a slip of paper stating '40 hours @ £1.40 = £56, less deduction 5 @ £1.20 = £50', after which any other deductions, such as tax and National Insurance, are listed.

There are other firms in the area employing women on light processes. Because of the possible exploitation of the women, a trade union is employing an organizer, Stella, to investigate the situation in each firm and, if possible, to recruit members.

Stella has learned that the normal hourly wage for light work – clothes machining, light assembly, packing – is £2.00 an hour. She has also found out about the lower rate and the payment system at L & L. Eventually Stella discovers a woman, Geraldine, who is willing to join the union and to recruit other members.

This recruitment is soon noticed by Oscar, who is not pleased, as he is afraid that he will be pressured to increase the women's wages. The recruitment is also far from popular with the forewoman, Betina, who is known to have accepted bribes to ensure that an applicant obtains a job. Oscar, while he does not know of Betina's corruption, is pleased to have her enthusiastic anti-union support.

Betina looks for a reason to dismiss Geraldine and thus bring the trade-union recruitment to an end. However, Geraldine is an excellent worker, neat, quick and accurate, and no fault can be found in her work.

Fay is 19 and was recruited to the work force eight weeks after Geraldine. Most of the women believe she is addicted to sniffing solvents and possibly even worse substances. She goes to the lavatory regularly to consume a can or two of beer and probably to sniff solvents. Her work is poor and her attendance unreliable.

It is commonplace for workers to be laid off as the needs of the business change. Staff taken on to meet seasonal demands are laid off when that demand slackens. Such a period now occurs and the company needs to discharge one of the making-up machinists. Betina selects Geraldine, although she has longer service and is acknowledged to be the best worker. As she tells Geraldine the news, Betina remarks, 'This will be good for you – you'll have plenty of time for your trade-union work.'

Geraldine goes to see Stella at once. She brings with her all her pay-slips and a few of the food vouchers. Stella consults the union, pointing out that because of Geraldine's activities there are now six members in the making-up workshop. The Branch Secretary finds the information, when coupled with clear evidence of the normal hourly rate in the town, most interesting. He writes to the union's legal adviser requesting her views on whether he should encourage Geraldine to

- complain about the hourly rate to the Senior Wages Inspector at the regional office of the Department of Employment

- refer the matter of the wage deductions to an industrial tribunal

- appeal to an industrial tribunal that she has been unfairly dismissed for trade-union membership and activity.

Within a week of Geraldine's dismissal Fay is dismissed for her bad workmanship, poor timekeeping and drunkenness.

Reference section

Oscar would have been well-advised to read *The Law on the Payment of Wages and Deductions*, which explains the Wages Act (Part I) of 1986.

Certainly the way in which the provision of food is put to the workers is important. Has the deduction been authorized by the worker's contract of employment or agreed by the worker in writing before it was made? If not, it is unlawful.

Betina's remark points to the strong possibility that Geraldine was dismissed for union activity. However, *Individual Rights of Employees* (pp. 9, 20) and *Fair and Unfair Dismissal* (p. 7) make it clear that dismissal for trade-union membership or union activity is unfair. There is apparently no evidence that Geraldine neglected her work for such activity. Had she done so the case would have been weakened, as a union must be recognized by an employer before its members may be allowed time off for union activities (see *Individual Rights of Employees* pp. 11, 12).

Before an industrial tribunal L & L would have to produce logical and reasonable criteria for Geraldine's redundancy rather than Fay's. This would be difficult, as Fay's subsequent dismissal shows that she was not regarded as an acceptable worker.

20 Buns & Buns Ltd

'Not a party to the agreement!'

Buns & Buns is a small bakery employing thirty people in the bakehouse and shop and on the bread rounds.

The founder of the business, Joe, had worked his way up from being a baker with a large company to owning this small, profitable business. Having been a loyal union member himself, he actually encouraged total membership. Just before his retirement in 1986 Joe and the union make a closed shop agreement in conformity with the law, and at the time of his retirement all the bakehouse staff, except Richard, were members of their appropriate union.

Richard is a very active and devout member of a religious sect that rejects trade-union membership as sinful. Because of this, Richard has never joined the union. Richard's refusal to join has been accepted by the small branch concerned as a legitimate conscientious objection, an acceptance made easier because of Richard's gentle and polite ways. He is, however, a solitary young man and takes little part in the conversations of his workmates.

Joe's retirement has resulted in management changes. Since Joe's children decided not to enter the trade, Joe's cousin Max has bought him out for a considerable sum. Max is faced with the heavy interest on the money he borrowed to buy out Joe and is determined to improve productivity. He therefore negotiates with the union and, by persuasion and creating the fear that otherwise the business might fail, obtains the branch's agreement to new terms. Their agreement states, 'As from 1 January 1986 all members of the Bakers' Union employed by Buns & Buns Ltd shall work in accordance with the shift patterns set out below.'

The agreement is implemented at once. Richard, however, appears to be oblivious to the new arrangements and turns up for work in accordance with the old shift rota. This innocent approach to the situation merely provokes laughter and initially his colleagues suggest that he be allowed to continue in his ways and given some separate tasks. However, this idea soon loses backing when it is made clear that Richard's work may well fall on other bakers. The shop steward begs Richard to join the union, is quietly rebuffed and abandons further efforts.

Richard is pressed to accept the new arrangements, but he explains that the old pattern enables him to attend to his many religious obligations and the new one will prevent this.

Max is not pleased. He has little sympathy for dissent in either bakery or religion and finds Richard's attitude laughable and outrageous. He, therefore, gives Richard a written notice to observe the new shift agreement. Richard mildly but firmly refuses and continues to work the previous shift pattern.

After further argument, Max gives Richard a letter stating that he is dismissed 'because of your repeated and determined failure to comply with the bakery agreement on shift working'. Richard, solitary as ever, leaves at once without speaking to his workmates. He is very upset about this dismissal, especially as unemployment is high and his three years with Buns & Buns have been happy and prosperous ones for him. He talks to his pastor, who suggests he talks to another member of the congregation, who is a solicitor. This man gets a copy of the agreement made by Max and the union. As it is clear to him that it is an agreement with union members only, and not with Richard, he writes to Max that he believes Richard has been unfairly dismissed.

Reference section

Richard's behaviour must seem unreasonable to Max and, indeed, to his workmates. This is usual when a minority refuses to participate in the arrangements made by the majority.

It can be argued that, in the long run, one of five things must happen:

1. Richard joins the union;
2. Richard accepts the agreement personally and in writing;
3. The agreement is revised to suit Richard;

Buns & Buns Ltd

4. Richard is found work to which the agreement does not apply – for example, as a roundsman or in a shop;
5. Richard must leave.

Richard has already rejected the first two options, and the third is an unlikely solution. The fourth option is perhaps the best, although Max may, for temperamental reasons, dislike it. However, if such an offer were made, Richard would probably place himself in a poor position to resist dismissal should he reject it.

As it is, Richard has been dismissed for a reason that might not be accepted by an industrial tribunal, since he cannot be a party to an agreement reached with a union of which he is not a member. Max needs to study the rules on closed shops in *Fair and Unfair Dismissal* (pp. 20, 21), which points out that the dismissal of a non-union member who will not join because of conscientious or religious conviction is unfair, as well as *Employment Acts 1980 and 1982*.

In the long run Richard may be dismissed, but the dismissal must arise from his failure to accept revised conditions that apply to him personally (see *Written Statement of Main Terms and Conditions of Employment*, p. 6). Alternatively, the employer could say that the dismissal was for another and substantial reason, such as reorganization or rationalization. If this explanation seemed logical, Richard could be in difficulty.

21 Fine Enamels PLC

'Pyrrhic victory'

Tom has recently joined this firm, which employs ninety full-time staff and specializes in enamelling processes. The principal works, where Tom is assistant works manager, has been plagued by a series of strikes. Officially, all the strikes have been caused by disputes over wages, bonus payments and working practices, but, in fact, the true cause lies in the extraordinary antipathy between Harold, the works manager, and Colin, the shop steward. Politically and personally, these two men clash on almost every occasion they meet, so that a poisonous atmosphere has started to spread through the works.

Both men are strong leaders. The hourly-paid personnel find Colin's incessant vigilance and willingness to harry the works manager a sign of his concern for their welfare. This attitude is reinforced by Harold's old-fashioned desire for formal respect and the sharpness, even harshness, of his speech.

All the management, with the exception of Tom, are over 45, most being in their late fifties. They tend to look back to times when 'there was more discipline and no messing about'. To them, therefore, Harold's style is acceptable and effective. They like his openly expressed view that trade unionists should be got rid of as soon as possible, 'by fair means or foul', as he was once heard to say.

Shortly after Tom's arrival a fresh crisis occurs. As so often happens, the spark that starts the conflagration is small and apparently insignificant. It has for some time been the practice for the effective working day to start at 8.30, although the actual official time is 8.15. The fifteen-minute interval is spent in drinking tea and coffee (prepared by the duty security officer, who starts work at 7.30) and general discussion. Harold has noticed that some men have been starting work as late as 8.45, attributes this to what he describes

Fine Enamels PLC

as general slackness and forbids the early morning ritual of tea and coffee drinking. Colin tries to raise the issue officially, but Harold refuses to see him.

Feeling is running high and Colin, after a brief consultation with members, instructs them to withdraw their labour. Harold refuses all discussion until there has been a return to work. Colin insists that there must be a return to the status quo before any return to work. Thus a deadlock occurs, made all the fiercer by the personal antipathy of the two men, which has grown steadily greater with each dispute.

The directors of the company are alarmed at the situation and hold an emergency meeting, at which the Company Secretary produces figures indicating a steady decline in the works' profitability. The directors decide to close down this factory and transfer all work, including outstanding orders, to the plant in Wales. Here the small labour force is largely non-union and there is ample space. Additional local labour is available, but will require training.

Organizing the closure and removal is entrusted to Harold, who is guaranteed the same job in Wales, since the works manager there is close to retirement. Excited beyond his usual taciturnity at the thought of the chagrin and dismay of his old enemy, Harold proposes the dismissal of all personnel, the re-engagement of those who are not involved in the strike and wish to go to Wales, and redundancy terms for those who do not wish to go. All the strikers are dismissed.

The board accepts this proposition and Tom, who also is guaranteed a job at the factory in Wales, is told to draw up the necessary letters to all concerned. So far Tom has not spoken, but now he points out that the recruitment of local labour will not be immediately effective, as training is essential before production can achieve the full volume. He also explains that one member of the strikers will be virtually irreplaceable. This man alone has skills in the heat-treatment and furnace-management part of the process, which have not yet been the subject of successful scientific analysis. True, he has an assistant, but to depend on his recently acquired skills at so crucial a moment would be hazardous. There is also the matter of training and here the experienced man's skills are important.

The Chairman's decision, supported by the other board members, is to discharge all the strikers, but to offer the skilled man to whom

Tom has referred and his assistant re-engagement at the Wales factory four or five days after the move. The Chairman also points out that as the strikers believe that the company is interested in a negotiated settlement, and as the annual shutdown of fourteen days is to begin in a week's time, the board should meet again in two days to finalize details.

Harold is instructed to produce a paper outlining the whole scheme. As he and Tom leave the boardroom, he remarks to Tom, 'A sheer bloody waste of time. I'll start making some inquiries as to possible costs of the move through some friends of mine, and you can get on with drafting the paper for the board. See you make them understand the need for a prompt decision on the lines the Chairman suggested.'

Tom is entirely untrained in personnel problems and his report concentrates on the technical aspects of the removal. His paper, which is largely a formalization of Harold's views and intentions, is accepted by the board. Thus on the Friday night preceding the annual shutdown period, a fleet of vehicles and industrial removal experts enter the factory, by the entrance from which all pickets have been withdrawn, and leave in a convoy for Wales on Saturday evening.

On Monday all the staff receive their various letters. Some of the non-strikers decide to accept redundancy terms and others, especially the younger men and women, decide to go to Wales. The strikers, stunned by their unexpected dismissal, arrange a meeting for the following Friday. At this meeting the two men the company wants to retain reveal that they have now received offers of re-employment in Wales and ask the other members to advise them. Cries of 'Don't be a bloody scab!' are silenced by the Regional Officer, who, to the members' surprise – but not Colin's – says, 'Take the re-engagement – accept it today. Don't worry. You'll see, it'll all work out right.'

When the firm reopens for business the two men start work in the factory in Wales. Shortly afterwards Tom is summoned to Harold's office. 'Well, your report on the arrangements and your daft ideas on re-engagement have certainly let us in for trouble. You'll be lucky to keep your job. We've just had an industrial tribunal "Notice of Appearance!"

Reference section

This case study again illustrates the danger of assuming that a dispute can be conducted without regard to the law and emphasizes the advisability of seeking advice before committing the company to a course of action that may lead to an expensive and embarrassing public hearing of disputes.

To understand why the Regional Officer advised the two men to accept re-engagement, read 'When is dismissal unquestionably unfair?' and *'Dismissal during an industrial dispute'* in *Fair and Unfair Dismissal. Industrial Action and the Law* contains the following useful summary:

> The 1982 Act introduced three safeguards for employers. It provided that, in order to avoid claims of unfair dismissal based on selective dismissal, the employer need treat in the same way only those who are taking part in the industrial action on a particular date and who are at the same establishment. At the same time it also provided that from three months after the date of dismissals, the employer may re-engage any of the dismissed employees without risking claims of unfair dismissal from employees not so re-engaged.

It appears that by re-engaging the two dismissed men the company has opened the way for the dismissed strikers to demand that they be treated as having been made redundant. Moreover, the union could complain to an industrial tribunal that the company had failed in its duty to consult, which could result in a Protective Award involving payment of employees for periods of between twenty-eight and ninety days (see *Redundancy Consultation and Notification*).

Whether it could be shown that the workers had been unfairly dismissed for industrial activity is less easy to decide. Perhaps this could arise from the firm's failure to offer the strikers, or as many as possible, re-engagement at the new works, as has been offered to other employees.

It must also be doubted whether anyone with such violent feelings as Harold should be entrusted with general management without a clear grasp of employment procedures; see App. II, The ACAS code, of the booklet *Fair and Unfair Dismissal*.

The firm now faces a hearing before an industrial tribunal unless conciliation is effective. It is necessary to read carefully the section beginning on p. 10 in *Fair and Unfair Dismissal* and give serious thought to the possibility of conciliation using the service provided by ACAS.

22 The Brass Man Ltd

'We can't let them cut our throats!'

You are Company Secretary of The Brass Man, which manufactures small motor vehicle spares. One of your customers is Beem's, a nation-wide distributor that sells parts to garages and spares retailers. The normal practice is for The Brass Man to supply the parts, which are primarily small, intricate brass castings, in bulk to Beem's central warehouse. There they are repacked into smaller boxes and sent to local centres from which both the trade and retailers are supplied.

Beem's is currently in dispute with the transport personnel and other staff at its central warehouse. In an effort to carry on its business, it has sent The Brass Man orders that, rather unusually, request direct delivery to various retailers, from whom the garages can also collect parts at trade prices.

When the trade unions at Beem's central warehouse discover what is happening, they attempt to organize secondary industrial action at The Brass Man's premises. Their efforts soon begin to show signs of success: your factory employees try to prevent the manufacture of parts to fill the Beem's orders that involve direct dispatch to retailers.

Since the parts The Brass Man makes go to more than one customer, it is difficult to differentiate between the goods for one customer and another during manufacture and handling. Therefore, the industrial action at your works has been gradually concentrated on the distribution aspect. When they have attempted to collect parts, your drivers have been persuaded to turn back. Although the purpose is to prevent goods being taken to retailers normally supplied by Beem's, because your transport vehicles usually carry loads for a number of customers this action has prevented the collection and delivery of orders that have nothing to do with that strike-bound customer.

To complicate matters, some of the retailers who are desperate for the parts The Brass Man makes have sent their own orders. They have never done this before, preferring to rely on the stocks carried by the large distributor rather than having working capital needlessly tied up since your company is unwilling to deal in small quantities. The fact that these retailers' orders have been received and acted upon by your company has greatly annoyed the strikers at Beem's, who are not only alarmed for the immediate cause but also can see that direct dealing with The Brass Man by retailers could lead to loss of business and consequent redundancy at Beem's.

Your own employees are in something of a dilemma. They have agreed to support the strike at your customer's central premises by trying to ensure that the distribution of parts to them is effectively halted. However, they can see that frustrating the effort of retailers to deal direct with you could be injurious to The Brass Man and to themselves. They therefore decide to continue with their action in respect of orders placed by Beem's but not to interfere with making parts and delivering them to satisfy orders placed directly with you by individual retailers.

This decision disturbs the strikers at Beem's and, encouraged by some very active branch members, they decide to picket The Brass Man's works with the intention of preventing the direct distribution of parts normally supplied to retailers by their firm. To do this they stand at your works entrance shouting and trying to stop goods vehicles entering and leaving.

At this point the directors of The Brass Man become very worried. This is a modest firm with only 100 employees but with an established reputation in a competitive trade. So far each year has shown better results, but the directors begin to fear that competitors, both home and foreign, could use any industrial disputes to their advantage. They call upon you to make a brief report and to let them know what remedies they might take before it is too late. As the Chairman remarks, 'If we're not careful, between them they may end by cutting our throats and theirs in a quarrel that is not of our making!'

You are a little worried, as you are an accountant and industrial disputes are not really your subject. However, the Works Manager, a recently promoted foreman, knows even less than you!

The Brass Man Ltd

Reference section

The problem facing you is that there is secondary industrial action at your works, which may be unlawful, and there is secondary picketing by people from your customer's warehouse, which appears to be illegal. You need to read *Employment Acts 1980 and 1982*, and to study pages 8–11 in particular. Consider carefully whether your own employees' secondary industrial action is lawful. The four conditions it must meet, which limit secondary industrial action and prevent it becoming indiscriminate, are:

1. the workers involved in secondary action work for a customer or supplier of the employer in dispute;
2. that supplier or customer has a current commercial contract with the employer in dispute;
3. the principal purpose of the secondary action is directly to prevent or disrupt supplies to or from the employer in dispute;
4. the secondary action is likely to achieve its purpose.

There is evidence that, by turning away collecting lorries, business in no way connected with the dispute has been frustrated. If that is so, then there is evidence of unlawful secondary industrial action.

So far as the picketing is concerned, it would seem to be unlawful, as those concerned are protesting at a place of work other than their own.

If, after your reading of the booklet, you conclude that your company is the victim of unlawful trade union activity, and persuasion fails to halt that activity, then you can take legal action. Before you embark on legal action, however, you could well seek the advice of ACAS.

23 Shoddy & Co. Ltd

'Can't lift it, Matty – I'm not that strong!'

Shoddy & Co. employs a total of forty people. Marlene, who has worked for the firm for three years, has been on maternity leave. She has been very careful to carry out all the correct procedures, finally notifying her employer at least twenty-one days in advance of the date of her expected return to work.

Prior to her maternity leave her normal work was sorting woollen garments into appropriate groups in the initial stages of the preparation of the reusable woollen waste called shoddy. Although not a particularly agreeable job it is not heavy work and Marlene found the company of twelve women of her own age cheerful and supportive, especially when it became known that she was pregnant. Her fellow workers thought of her as being nice and rather genteel, but the supervisor found her 'disdainful'.

In her absence Marlene's place was taken by Angelina, a niece of one of the mill foremen. Angelina soon proved a good and energetic worker; and, being far more muscular and robust than Marlene, she worked at a pace that would have been beyond Marlene's strength. This increased productivity was not really very well received at first by her colleagues, but her enormous high spirits prevented the matter becoming the subject of quarrels or a dispute.

The sorting room forewoman has found Angelina very useful, as on a number of occasions she proved willing and able to undertake work that hitherto had had to be done by a strong man. Added to this, she finds that Angelina's extrovert ways and sense of humour match her own temperament whereas Marlene was, in her view, too quiet and prim. 'She felt she was a cut above us,' she once remarked.

In due course Marlene returns to work. She has heard about Angelina but, in the absence of any word to the contrary, she expects to have her old job given to her. On arrival at the mill, however, she finds that this is not to be. In a rather difficult interview the Mill Manager explains that instead of returning to the sorting floor, Marlene is to assist with the process by which the woollen rags are torn up. This work is dirty and dusty and it requires some strength to move the material from the sorting floor and tip it into the machines that tear it up. The work has always been done by a man and a youth, but the latter has left to join the army. The man is a veteran and has become so habituated to the work that he sees no disadvantages to it.

Marlene is very distressed. Instead of the company of friendly women her own age, with whom she could have talked about the baby, she is alone in a dirty room with a taciturn, rather scruffy, elderly man who usually smells strongly of the rags, beer and strong shag tobacco. Matty, the old man, is not at ease either. He is not an unkind man and, indeed, is a devoted grandfather, but he has never faced working with a young woman before. Moreover, despite his vigorous rejection of any suggestions about the matter, he does suffer from some degree of arthritis and relies on the presence of a strong companion. The lad who has joined the army and the others before him were usually pleased to demonstrate their strength by doing the heavier work.

To make matters worse, neither Matty nor Marlene has been warned of the fact that they are to work together. This is because the Mill Manager is not happy with the situation and wishes he had not agreed to hiring Angelina and, even more, that he had not agreed to her staying on the sorting floor. He has rather weakly drifted into the situation because of pressure from Angelina's uncle and the sorting-floor forewoman.

A crisis arises within three days of Marlene's return. Poor Matty's arthritis is playing him up and he asks Marlene to do some heaving and tipping, which pains him when he attempts it. Marlene makes an attempt – not perhaps a very willing or vigorous attempt – and then says, 'It's no good, Matty, I can't do it. I can't lift it. I'm not that strong, I have to think of the baby. What if I injure myself and can't look after him?'

The Mill Manager arrives on the scene. Poor Matty is upset that his own physical weakness is now revealed, the more so since he is 66 and fears he may be asked to retire. Marlene is distressed and filled with a sense of injustice. She bursts into tears, saying, 'You've got to give me my proper job back.'

The Mill Manager does the necessary heaving and lifting himself to get the work restarted and then goes back to his office and telephones the Jobcentre for advice.

Reference section

The crisis has developed, as so often happens, because of a lack of foresight and courage on the part of the person responsible – in this case the Mill Manager. By endeavouring to please two supervisors he has placed the company in a difficult legal position if Marlene decides to claim that she has, in effect, been unfairly dismissed.

The Mill Manager's first action should be to read *Individual Rights of Employees*, pp. 14–15, *Employment Rights for the Expectant Mother*, and *Fair and Unfair Dismissal*, pp. 17–18. These passages make it clear that a woman who has correctly carried out all the procedures required in connection with maternity leave and return to work is entitled to return to her original job unless that job no longer exists because of redundancy or it is not practicable for her to be reinstated for some other reason. In such cases she has to be offered a suitable alternative job. If the employer fails to give her either her old job or a suitable alternative, the employee is regarded as having been dismissed and may make a complaint of unfair dismissal to an industrial tribunal.

Marlene has carried out the necessary procedures and her original job exists, but she has not been reinstated. No question of redundancy appears to arise and, as it has more than five employees, Shoddy cannot claim that its size prevents Marlene's reinstatement or the offer of an alternative job.

As Marlene has been offered a different job, the only question is whether she is refusing, or is about to refuse, a *suitable* alternative. However, it appears that her new job is in no way equivalent and is unsuitable because of the physical demands it makes on her. Some conciliatory action seems to be indicated.

24 Finery Ltd

'No place for a man'

Finery Ltd is a retailer of high quality clothing for women. It sells not only dresses, blouses and skirts, but also a range of expensive coats, including imitation furs, some of which are of exceptionally good quality. In addition the shop stocks underwear, hosiery, gloves and costume jewellery. There are twelve sales staff in the shop in addition to the owner/manageress, four buyers, a cashier and wages clerk and a general assistant whose duty is to make coffee and tea for customers.

Edwin, who is 28, has worked for Finery for six years and is the buyer for coats. Before joining the firm he worked in the coats department of a very well-known department store, which he joined after he left school with five O levels. He subsequently attended a day-release course at a technical college and has a recognized qualification in retailing. However, it is not his qualifications alone that have raised him to the position as Coat Buyer, but his almost instinctive skill in this work. He had become an Assistant Buyer by the time he was 19 and left the department store on good terms; at that time there was no immediate prospect of promotion for him. The store's General Manager said when he left, 'Well, Ed, we hope you'll be back with us before too long.' Edwin keeps in touch with him.

When Edwin joined Finery, the firm was owned by a well-known and highly respected family, the head of which treated Edwin very much as a son. The old man was pleased to have the advice of a younger man and also valued his presence because the rest of the staff were women.

In this atmosphere Edwin flourished. However, disaster was not far off. The owner suffered a heart attack and was advised by his physician to retire; he was, in fact, 75 years old. Following this advice, the old man sold his business for a very considerable sum and bought a house in Cheshire, where he now lives. Edwin is a frequent visitor. Of late the old man has discussed with Edwin his plans to finance one of his daughters in a boutique not far from his old shop.

The new owner of the business is a clever, dominant 38-year-old woman who has considerable experience in retailing. This lady, Bella, does not like men and her natural ability and family wealth have given her great confidence, so she feels equal to any challenge except that provided by someone like Edwin, who after years of being the favourite of the old owner has come to have as high a regard for his own judgement as Bella has for hers. Their initial relations are little more than civil and Edwin rashly assumes a rather patronizing style.

Before long there is a fatal clash. One of Bella's friends, a somewhat temperamental person, comes to the shop to buy a fur coat. She had not realized that Edwin has stocked only artificial furs. He has done so because he has ethical doubts about the fur trade and because Finery's younger clientele, in particular, have turned away from real skins to synthetic fibres. When Bella's friend learns that no real furs are stocked she makes some highly critical remarks to Edwin, including 'I shouldn't think you'll be here long; Bella doesn't like fellows of your cocky type!' Edwin's response is not very tactful: 'I'm sorry we can't help you. Some people are hard to fit, of course, even when one has a range of natural furs.' The customer takes this as a mortal insult and refers the matter to Bella when she gets home.

Later the same day a customer is considering buying a coat and a dress. She has taken both items to the changing room and has put on the coat over her own dress. She doubts the competence of the saleswoman and demands that the buyer attend her. The saleswoman goes out, finds Edwin and brings him back to the changing room. The saleswoman knocks on the door, says 'I've brought the buyer, madam' and receives the reply, 'Come in.' While the saleswoman has been away, the customer has removed her dress in order to put on the dress she is considering buying. When Edwin enters she is, therefore, less than fully clad. Her shrieks of indignation echo through the shop, as she claims to be the victim of a gross insult to her modesty. Edwin is embarrassed by her reaction and leaves immediately, followed by threats.

The next morning Edwin is summoned by Bella, who, in the presence of the cashier, states briskly that she has had two complaints about his behaviour, one that he is incompetent and insolent and the other directed not at him personally, as the complainant, on reflection, recognizes that he meant no harm, but against the shop for employing a man.

'It is clear to me,' says Bella, 'that there is no place for you here and accordingly I am giving you written notice of dismissal because I do not think that as a man you can be employed to deal with customers in a woman's clothes shop – personally I can't think why you wish to!' She goes on, 'I am giving you two months' salary in lieu of notice and I should like you to leave at once.'

Edwin, although upset, tries to respond but his efforts to explain himself are met with the words, 'I've nothing against you personally, but you're a man, though you can't help that, and have no place here. Please don't argue. You occupy a specifically feminine job and what's more, I don't believe you've any loyalty to me!'

Edwin goes home and telephones his old employer, who is very unhappy at the turn events have taken. He telephones his lawyer and later phones Edwin to tell him that he should consider making a claim for unfair dismissal by reason of sex discrimination. 'Don't worry,' he says, 'my lawyer will sort it out for you.'

Edwin is worried, for he sees danger to his career whatever happens, but he goes to see the lawyer.

Reference section

It is a common error to think that only women can be victims of sex discrimination. This case study concerns possible sex discrimination against a man; to understand it fully read the relevant parts of the booklet *Sex Discrimination Act 1975*, in particular pp. 8 (paragraph 3.6), 10–11 (especially paragraph 3.13) and 40–5.

If this case were to go before a tribunal Bella would find it difficult to justify Edwin's dismissal since the incident involving the customer who wanted natural fur does not by itself justify dismissal, while in the second incident, which presumably is the one used to justify Edwin's dismissal on sexual grounds, Edwin did not behave improperly.

Bella may be claiming that a genuine occupational qualification exists in respect of the showroom staff of her shop and that she is entitled to dismiss Edwin on this basis. However, as the booklet makes clear, provided there were enough female assistants to cover changing-room duties the requirement on the employer not to discriminate would apply to the other jobs.

Finally, study 'Dismissal on Transfer of an Undertaking' in the booklet *Fair and Unfair Dismissal* (p. 20). It would be difficult to use the transfer of this business as a reason for Edwin's dismissal unless Bella can show such a degree of non-discriminatory reorganization as might justify such an action. As for Edwin's alleged disloyalty it would be very hard to prove.

25 Switchon PLC

'It's a woman's work!'

You have just been appointed Works Manager of Switchon, which manufactures specialized electrical switchgear. It is a small firm with an excellent record of labour relations. The Chairman, Managing Director and principal shareholder is a good engineer, a sound organizer and an astute businessman, but is liable to become overconcerned with small matters, which he elevates to the level of principles for which he will risk confrontation.

The individual items produced are small, extremely complicated and very expensive. They are designed by your company in accordance with the requirements of individual customers and the manufacture is carried out by skilled technicians. These technicians are mainly men but there are some women. All are paid at the same rate.

The company is receiving a great deal of business from home and overseas buyers, usually governed by very strongly emphasized delivery requirements. Your company produces what is generally accepted as the best product available, but rival organizations are fast catching up in respect of quality. One competitor in particular is offering rather better delivery times.

For dispatch to customers the switchgear is packed in very strong cardboard boxes and packing materials are used to prevent its movement in the box. For some years the work of packing and preparing goods for dispatch has been carried out by men who have been regarded as semi-skilled and usually have been older than the technicians. The reason for this is that originally Switchon's product was of a nature that enabled much of the manufacture to be done by semi-skilled labour. When the product was changed some ten years ago to the present individually designed and highly specialized type, those semi-skilled men who so wished were retained as packers. This was a compassionate decision by the former chairman, who had known many of these men from their youth.

These packers' tasks consisted of selecting and collecting suitable boxes from the stores. They then assembled these boxes, which were supplied in a flat form, packed them with the equipment and labelled them.

Just before you joined the firm four of the six packers reached an age when they could retire. This should have been foreseen but was not. Your predecessor appointed four unskilled women to replace the retiring men and reorganized the work. Your predecessor took the view that much time was wasted when the packing was broken off to go to the stores, and that time was being misspent in unskilled work by the technicians, who needed more support by labourers. Therefore he decided that the four women were to spend all their time in setting up the boxes, fetching the packing material and packing the switchgear. The two remaining men were assigned to collecting the flat boxes from the stores and general labouring within the factory. The wage rates of the men were to continue as before. New rates were decided on for the women workers and accepted by them. These rates were significantly lower than those paid to the men.

Shortly after you arrived one of the men was found to be physically unfit for some of the new labouring duties, while at the same time four packers were not able to cope with increased output. The unfit man was returned to packing, and a Training Commission trainee given the job of collecting boxes and general labouring along with the remaining male labourer.

It so happens that one of the newly-appointed women workers is related to the unfit man, and before long she becomes aware of the fact that the packers in the past were, and the one male packer who is continuing to collect his own boxes is, paid £3 a week more, gross, than the women.

The company is virtually completely unionized and the women take their case to the convenor, who seeks an appointment with you. At this meeting the convenor points out that the company is in breach of the Equal Pay Act and asks for the women to be paid at the same rate as the man.

You have asked the convenor to wait until you have spoken to the Chairman. Rather to your surprise the Chairman refuses to consider

Switchon PLC

paying the women at the same rate as the man. His argument is that there has always been a distinction between men and women's work, and the fact that there is a difference between the duties of male packers – in the past and at present in the case of the remaining man – and the duties of the women proves his point. 'Even though he's not fit, he still does something different,' says the Chairman.

He winds up the discussion by claiming that he has plans for adding a new range of products to the firm's catalogue that, like those in the distant past, can be assembled by semi-skilled labour. 'We'll look pretty daft if we have to pay unskilled assembly staff the same rate as semi-skilled workers.'

You do not feel that a return to the convenor with this news will prove useful and you are right. He points out that the Chairman does not understand the law, and adds that since the company is tied to strict delivery dates a 'go slow' and 'work to rule' by the angry women would be unhelpful to all.

The ball is now back in your court and you need to return to the Chairman with a clearly reasoned set of arguments based on the law.

Reference section

Your first task will be to study the booklet *Equal Pay – A Guide to the Equal Pay Act*, and Section 11, 'Like Work', in particular. This makes clear that a woman is employed on like work to that of a man when she is doing the same work or work broadly similar. It is doubtful that the difference at your firm's packing department is significant.

The immediate cost to the company will be £12 a week. True, the setting up of a much larger packing department at those rates might produce a larger 'loss'. However, this future situation remains speculative, and if the packing were then to be organized in a radically different way from that currently prevailing, it could be that any attempt to quote the present situation as a precedent would fail.

In certain circumstances, when employees are transferred to less skilled work that would normally carry less pay, they have their previous rate specially preserved. A tribunal could consider if this is the case here, as in such circumstances the difference in pay would not be considered related to a difference in sex. However, tribunals always scrutinize such arrangements very carefully to make sure they are genuine. Moreover they should not be permanent and it is doubtful whether this argument could be advanced by the company.

In considering the problem and advising the Chairman, there is another important matter to be considered: hitherto your company has had an enviable relationship with its branch of the trade union. This is now being jeopardized.

The Chairman may well feel that a principle is involved, but nothing that he may think can over-ride the law and a tribunal's decision could go against the company.

26 Electro Gadgets PLC

'Girls don't play rugger!'

You are the Managing Director of Electro Gadgets, which designs and manufactures electronic devices in accordance with the detailed requirements of specific customers. The company employs sixty people in the design, manufacture and assembly of the equipment, and an office and sales staff of twenty-five.

Electro Gadgets' products are extensively advertised and business is obtained by following up inquiries, through contacts and by some canvassing by letter, telephone and visits. There is no telephone sales policy as generally understood, as the directors consider the nature of the product to be too confidential to be dealt with by open cold canvassing. The direct approaches to possible customers are, therefore, left to the sales force acting as experience, training and their personal characters indicate.

There are five 'internal' sales staff, four of whom are women, headed by the Sales Office Manager, also a woman. Their job is to liaise between the customers and both the design and manufacturing staff and the technical representatives, service inquiries by telephone or letter, and perform other office-bound sales-orientated activities. They are not paid very highly since the work requires little technical knowledge and is mainly a matter of patience, good manners and prompt response.

There are ten external sales staff, the technical representatives. They are well paid: their basic salary is £10,000 a year, and their commission on sales is such that the minimum total income they can expect is over £15,000; in fact, five of the salesmen habitually receive more than £20,000.

The word 'salesmen' is used correctly, for all the technical representatives are men. They are recruited widely and include ex-service personnel with an understanding of security problems, former police officers, former electronics design office staff, and salesmen experienced in the sale of electronically based consumer durables such as reprographic equipment, computers and the like. They receive thorough training on recruitment and are constantly sent on courses and to specialist conferences and other gatherings of that kind to update their knowledge. From time to time members of the sales office are transferred to field sales work; applicants usually take a basic sales course provided by a firm of sales consultants for the company.

It is well known in the company that within six months two of the external sales staff – men in their early fifties – will retire; speculation develops as to whether there will be any internal promotion. Knowing that there is to be a basic sales training course in the immediate future, two members of the sales office staff apply.

One of them is Hugo, the only male member of the internal sales team, and the other is Myfanwy, also one of the internal sales team.

Hugo is 25 years old, holds a modest business studies qualification and, after a few false starts elsewhere, has been employed in Electro Gadgets for four years. He is an agreeable young man with an engaging air of candour and honesty. His work has been commented on favourably by the Sales Office Manager, who regards him as reliable rather than persistent and determined. He is a keen sportsman and plays rugby for a club to which several of the external sales force belong.

Myfanwy is a graduate in business studies, who joined Electro Gadgets immediately after completing her studies when she was 21. She too has spent four years with the company. Myfanwy is intelligent, alert and possessed of simple but engaging good manners. Her work is well regarded by the Sales Office Manager, who has commented on her drive and persistence.

The decision as to who goes on the courses belongs to the company's Sales Director, who takes direct responsibility for the external sales force. This man, Monty, is in his late forties. He has worked in sales since he left school, beginning as a junior and eventually becoming Sales Director of Electro Gadgets. He has no formal training, but is very quick in picking up the essentials of any case he has to present. Moreover, he has been particularly zealous about attending courses and conferences throughout his career. Quick-witted, determined, presentable and very well-informed, he has an excellent relationship with the design staff and has proved extremely successful.

As part of his management style, the members of Monty's sales team have always been very close and pride themselves on their loyalty to each other, made easier by his strict territorial allocation of duties. They drink together copiously in weekly sessions and maintain a highly 'male chauvinist', 'Gung ho', team-game-playing life-style.

The course that Hugo and Myfanwy have applied to attend is expensive. It involves residence at a good hotel for sales training by a consultant, followed by intensive in-house technical training covering Electro Gadgets' products and those of rival firms. Both Hugo and Myfanwy are recommended for the course by their manager.

When the two applications come before him, Monty accepts Hugo's and rejects Myfanwy. Myfanwy is greatly disappointed and is not pleased when Monty puts his arm round her shoulders and says, 'My dear, you really shouldn't try to break into this kind of work – it's simply not your scene. Have you thought of entering Further Education? You'd do well there. After all, you don't like rugger, do you?'

Myfanwy broods over what has happened and when, three weeks later, an advertisement for two sales staff appears in the press and an official notice of impending vacancies in the sales force is sent round the office, she applies for one of the jobs. She is not placed on the short list but Hugo and two external candidates are. One of the external candidates and Hugo are appointed.

Myfanwy is very upset and casually visiting a Jobcentre she comes across the Home Office booklet *Sex Discrimination – A Guide to the Sex Discrimination Act 1975*. She has been aware of the act generally, but not of its specific provisions and how they affect her. She now reads the booklet carefully and comes to the conclusion that she has been discriminated against. Myfanwy considers what she should do and decides to make a complaint to an industrial tribunal. She informs her manager of her decision, and the matter is brought to your attention.

Reference section

As Managing Director, you should follow Myfanwy's example and read the booklet *Sex Discrimination – A Guide to the Sex Discrimination Act 1975*, especially p. 8, paragraph 3.6 (see p. 24 of this book); pp. 10–11, which lay down the rules by which a 'genuine occupational qualification' that effectively excludes one sex can be established; and Chapter 9, particularly p. 42, which deals with conciliation.

It is easy to see that Monty has built up his sales team by selecting people of suitable ability who conform to the social pattern he has established. This in itself is not illegal. All team builders try to ensure that team members are acceptable to one another, share certain interests and activities or cheerfully tolerate styles to which they do not want to conform.

However, it cannot be said that there is any possibility of establishing a genuine occupational qualification that would preclude a woman, on the basis of her sex, from selling electronic equipment or being trained to do so. Therefore, since both Hugo and Myfanwy have been recommended for training and on balance Myfanwy seems better qualified educationally and personally, it could be argued that she is being discriminated against. This seems to be confirmed by Monty's comments to her.

Myfanwy might do well to approach the Equal Opportunities Commission (EOC), which can assist and represent individual complainants, conduct investigations and issue non-discrimination notices.

The management also needs to read the booklet *Equal Pay – A Guide to the Equal Pay Act* and note particularly p. 16, paragraph 59, which describes the role of the EOC.

Whatever action you decide to take to redress Myfanwy's complaint, perhaps with the aid of a conciliation officer from ACAS, you will also need to discuss with the Sales Director his part in the story. Perhaps he needs some training himself to understand current employment legislation.

27 Boxes Ltd

'It came as a surprise'

Boxes Ltd has been operating for some years using hand tools and hand-controlled machinery. One process consists of cutting small diamond-shaped patterns on the flat surface of precious metals used in the production of small vessels. The machine used in this process requires the skilful operation of its controls as faulty operation can easily ruin sheets of precious metal.

Recently a machine that can carry out the work semi-automatically has come on the market. After much consideration, including calculating that the new machine will result in such savings that the company can reduce its prices, the directors of Boxes Ltd decide to purchase one machine.

One of the three people currently using the old machines has to be chosen for training in setting up the new machine, thus eventually leaving the other two without work and therefore likely to be redundant. Although the firm does not operate a closed shop, it has recognized a union, the Ornamental Boxmakers' Union, a small organization operating mainly in those towns having an assay office. It so happens that only one of the three employees concerned is a member of the union. The others do not belong to any union.

In order to gain a march on their competitors the directors order the machine for very early delivery and at once start to consider the choice of the operator to be trained. Of the three people concerned, two are extremely conservative in their approach to change and the third, the union member, is most adaptable and willing to learn. The directors decide to make the two non-union members redundant and to send the union member to the supplier's factory, to be retrained in preparation for the delivery of the firm's new machine.

Because of the competition with rival firms the directors have decided on a policy of secrecy and they do not make any move to tell the two redundant employees or the person to be retrained of their decision until the last possible moment. Therefore, when they call in and announce their plans to these employees, all three are surprised and the two being made redundant are indignant. Their redundancy pay due has already been worked out and they are given three weeks' notice of termination of employment, as required by their three years' service.

The union member, though pleased to have been selected to operate the new machine, is unhappy about the fate of his two colleagues and consults his union. There the news is not well received and very shortly afterwards the union writes to the company that it is in breach of the law and may be the subject of a complaint to an industrial tribunal.

The directors are surprised and unhappy, as they feel that they have been correct in their procedures and in their treatment of their workers. To try to understand the situation they ask the union representative to call to see them.

Reference section

This problem arises from the fact that what seems fair to the directors is not necessarily so and in any event does not comply with current industrial legislation. The directors should have read the booklets *Redundancy Consultation and Notification*, especially p. 5, and *Individual Rights of Employees*, particularly p. 21.

If they had done so, they would have known that when redundancy is contemplated, the union recognized by the employer – in this case the Ornamental Boxmakers' Union – must first be consulted by the employer even when the individuals to be made redundant are not members and even when they volunteer for redundancy. The notice to be given to the union is defined by law and although no specific period is laid down when fewer than ten employees are concerned, the consultation *must* occur.

As it is, the union may ask a tribunal to make a Protective Award, which will require the company to pay the employees their normal weekly wage for a period determined by the tribunal in the light of the circumstances. The maximum periods are defined on pp. 7–8 of the redundancy booklet; it would be twenty-eight days in this case.

Had ten or more people been made redundant, the company would have been subject to more stringent rules about the notice to be given to the union and compulsory notification, under penalty for default, to the Department of Employment.

28 Stones and Settings Ltd

'I wish I could employ you!'

Clarice, a brilliant jewellery designer, owns a small jewellery business. She has recently received news that her diamond expert is retiring rather earlier than expected in order to take over a well-established and very successful jeweller's shop in North Wales. This he hopes eventually to hand over to his son, who, though a skilled jeweller, is more interested in retailing than manufacture.

Clarice advertised the vacancy in the trade journals and there have been only three applicants who are worth considering. They are Santokh, Frances and Hans.

Santokh is a young man just out of his apprenticeship. He has a sound reputation and good references from his college. Frances is rather older, but still lacking experience. Hans is the oldest and has excellent references from former employers. His application states that he had his own business but had been forced to give it up during a long period of recovery from a motor accident.

All three applicants are interviewed. Santokh turns out to be an admirable young man, lacking only in experience to take up so responsible a job. Frances is a very keen and intelligent young woman. Like Santokh, she has a good college record and excellent references, but lacks experience.

Hans produces something of a shock. He is a man in his mid-thirties, whose German father and Dutch mother are naturalized British citizens. Hans was born and went to school in Britain, and speaks English and German equally well. Hans has never married and lives a rather enclosed though happy life with his parents. As a jeweller specializing in precious stones he is, according to reports, really extremely gifted.

The shock occurs when he arrives in a car with hand controls and disembarks into a wheelchair. Clarice's business is conducted in the

Stones and Settings Ltd

upper part of an old building and approached by a staircase with no landing that leads straight into the workshop. A couple of offices have been partitioned at one end of the room. The precious stones are kept in a small safe cemented into the wall and so secured that explosives would be necessary to remove it quickly. There is an iron fire escape to the rear, leading to a yard. Downstairs is a firm specializing in silverware, with whose owner Clarice is friendly.

Having arrived, Hans has to be interviewed and this is conducted in the silversmith's workshop. Originally started as a courtesy, the interview ends with Clarice in some perplexity. She realizes that in Hans she has an opportunity to employ a most gifted jeweller but on the other hand she cannot see how she can accommodate someone in a wheelchair.

Distressed and frustrated she explains the problem to Hans, who proves very understanding and unresentful, and explains that the compensation he received for his injuries is well invested. They part on good terms and Clarice promises to give his name to anyone she hears of who has more suitable premises.

Clarice then reconsiders Santokh and Frances. She phones Santokh at his home and finds that he is no longer looking for a job. His present employer, suspecting his intention to leave and, like Clarice, having an impending vacancy, has decided to promote him.

Next she speaks to Frances. Here she is also disappointed. Frances has been offered work at the jewellery college, initially as a part-time member of staff, but with every indication that her chances of full-time employment are very good. Aware of some degree of prejudice against women in workshops, she has decided to take a chance and work for the college.

Disappointed, Clarice readvertises. None of the resulting applicants seems up to the standard of Hans, Frances or Santokh.

Reference section

This rather melancholy story is an example of the fact that many of the benefits available to individuals and organizations are not taken up through ignorance of their existence. It also indicates the way in which disabled people are, perhaps, 'written off' without very much thought.

Hans is fortunate that the compensation he received keeps him from poverty, but nevertheless he may soon feel bored and frustrated.

Had Clarice read the booklet *Employing Disabled People – Sources of Help*, she could probably have employed Hans to their mutual advantage. She would have discovered not only lists of very useful addresses but also that grants of up to £6,000 can be made to help an employer to recruit or retain a specific disabled person. Other grants and benefits are listed and the booklet repays reading.

29 Artistic Products Ltd

'Bodily fluids'

Artistic Products Ltd makes and sells decorative glassware. The small staff of ten craftsmen and women and five office and sales staff operate a thriving business, part retail – they have a small shop in a shopping centre – and part wholesale, selling their goods to large department stores and up-market gift shops.

All the pieces are handmade. The craftsmen and women have usually had some kind of artistic training and have turned to glass as a medium that they find especially satisfying. Because of their similar backgrounds, they form an intimate community supportive of, and interested in, one another's work.

There are six craftsmen, all in their mid-twenties and early thirties. Three of them are married and have children; one is married and hoping to start a family soon; one lives with his girl-friend, who is pregnant, and one is a bachelor. Three of the craftswomen are in the same age range as the men, while the fourth, Ann, is an especially gifted person of about 45. One of the women is engaged, while Ann and the other two women are married and have children, and Ann is a grandmother.

The office and sales staff comprise an office manager, a woman of 35, two clerk/typists, and two sales representatives, one running the shop and one travelling.

Artistic Products was founded by Ann, who is now the Managing Director, and her husband, Glyn, who is also a director and runs the shop. The third director is Adam, who was engaged as a craftsman designer from the start of the business.

Unhappily, this hitherto harmonious community has been torn apart by the issue of AIDS. It has always been known that George, the bachelor craftsman, who also has been with the company from its inception, has a bisexual private life. This has always been tolerated by the others until it was learned that George is a carrier of HIV, the virus that causes AIDS.

Pam, one of the craftswomen, has a close friend (not a colleague) who has been to her in great distress for advice. This friend has been engaged in a sexual relationship with George, has discovered his homosexuality and, noticing that he seemed particularly upset, has forced from him a confession of his medical condition. Pam has reassured her to some extent by pointing out that the fact that she insisted on the use of a condom makes the chances of her being infected very small indeed.

Having reassured her friend as far as possible, Pam then considers whether or not she should communicate her knowledge to her colleagues. Even after much agitated thought, the study of a leaflet and a talk with one of the counselling services, she remains unsure. At last she decides to confide in Millie, who is a close, lifelong friend and a colleague.

Pam and Millie spend that evening discussing the issue with their male partners. They consider in particular the nature of the craft process in which they are engaged. Working with glass and using no protective gloves, they are all exposed to the risk of occasional cuts and, because of the use of heat, of blisters arising from minor burns. Blowpipes are also used and these are each normally handled by one person. Nevertheless, both women can recall occasions when they have mistakenly used a blowpipe other than their own. The news of George's condition is especially disturbing to Millie, who is pregnant with her second child. After long and rather perplexed argument, the four agree that all the staff must know.

Because George is a courteous and helpful colleague neither Pam nor Millie can bear the thought of, as they put it, 'denouncing him'. They, therefore, explain the situation to Ann. She receives the news with genuine horror and at once consults her husband, and fellow director, Glyn. They decide to ask Millie and Pam to remain silent for another forty-eight hours, made easier by the coming weekend.

Ann immediately begins to study the accident book, which she has always insisted be meticulously kept. It shows that during the last twelve months George, always a very quick worker, has burnt his left hand twice, raising what are described as 'nasty broken blisters', and cut his fingers on four occasions, one sufficiently serious as to warrant the note 'lots of blood – went to hospital for tetanus injection'. Ann discusses these facts with Glyn and Adam, whose wife is hoping to start a family soon. They come to the conclusion that on these occasions George must have emitted bodily fluids from the blisters and the cuts. They also take into consideration that the virus has been found in saliva. Over the weekend they continue to make inquiries and discover that the local fire brigade and ambulance service have been issued with devices to avoid mouth-to-mouth contact with persons needing resuscitation. An article in a reliable newspaper adds to their fears by stating that the spilt blood of HIV carriers and AIDS sufferers should be treated with bleach and carefully mopped up.

All of them are anxious and distressed. George is a pleasant man and a valued member of the team, but the directors are very concerned about the posibility of endangering other staff and their families, and in Glyn a well-concealed but still strong distaste for homosexual practices begins to prevail.

Unfortunately, Pam and Millie take the forty-eight hour limit very literally. On Monday morning, in the absence of George, who has gone to a museum to look at some glass objects, they tell the others about his condition. The reactions range from calm acceptance to extreme fear, with the fearful in the majority. Just as the three directors are bracing themselves to deal with the situation, they are met by the staff, of whom all but two demand George's dismissal. While these representations are being made George arrives and learns what has happened.

Under considerable pressure and in deep sorrow, the directors interview George, who points out that he is still well and may continue so, and that he has abstained and will continue to abstain from all sexual activity. As this conversation is going on there is a knock on the door and a letter is handed in from the craft staff explaining that unless George leaves they, excepting the two dissenters, will resign immediately. Such a step would destroy the company.

The directors ask George to remain in the office and withdraw to another room. There they decide to discharge George on medical grounds and to make him an *ex gratia* gift of £5,000. This decision is conveyed to George there and then, orally and in writing. He is asked to leave the premises at once but is told he will be given, in addition to the £5,000, three months' full salary in lieu of notice. The rest of the staff are told of the decision as they notice George driving off.

A few days later Ann receives a telephone call from a lawyer suggesting that his client, George, has been unfairly dismissed, but that he might be willing to accept a worthwhile sum in compensation.

Reference section

This sad story is an instance of the truth that management decisions are basically ethical decisions, although the ethical basis is often overclouded by economic and 'political' factors. In this case the facts on which to base a decision are hard to come by. Since the nature of HIV and AIDS is not fully known, it follows that decisions taken may be wrong.

It has been stated at Cabinet Minister level that infection with HIV is not a reason for dismissal, but this generalized statement may admit of exceptions. By analogy one may ask should an employer continue the employment of a person suffering from such a disease as pulmonary tuberculosis in its infectious stage?

The answer to the question in respect of George is that the degree of danger to fellow employees is not known. The decision to discharge him has clearly been taken for two reasons. First, the fact that the nature of the work is such that bodily fluids may be transferred, and, second, the virtual refusal of other staff to work with him.

It is noteworthy that no effort has been made to provide George with work to minimize the risk to others as perceived by the directors and staff. Should he attempt to pursue a claim for compensation through an industrial tribunal, the absence of such an attempt may well count against the company.

Before matters develop further the directors should read the booklet *AIDS and Employment*, which gives advice and lists various helpful organizations. They should pay special attention to paragraph 7 because it could be argued that the precautions mentioned therein make clear the possible dangers in a workshop such as that of Artistic Products. Paragraphs 8 to 11 point out the need to consider the possibility of a move to other duties or alternative employment, for example, in the shop.

This case study again illustrates the need to avoid making rapid and ill-thought-out decisions under pressure.

30 News & Food PLC

'But they love working for me!'

Hussain is a thoroughly vigorous entrepreneur. From very small beginnings, with the aid of bank loans, he has built up a thriving newsagent's business, and now he has purchased the shop next door. It is of very considerable size and Hussain has started a restaurant and take-away service in one half, and a small self-service store in the other.

Hussain is a very well-organized person and, having had one of his brothers nearly die of food poisoning, he is very scrupulous about cleanliness and good order in all matters affecting food. He is a law-abiding man providing he is aware of what the law demands. Thus, because he wishes to slaughter poultry on his premises in accordance with Islamic dietary rules, he has taken the advice of a lawyer friend and been careful to obtain the permission of the authorities, who are well satisfied with the general hygiene of his premises.

Business is thriving. The quality of food provided by his restaurant has attracted favourable notice and his self-service store is well supported. The original business, the newsagent's, has also increased its turnover. Hussain has paid particular attention to newspaper deliveries and his customers are more than satisfied with the accuracy and regularity of his service. Those who start off early for work are especially pleased by the fact that papers arrive just after 6.30 a.m.

The busy period in the restaurant and take-away is from about 8.30 p.m. until 12.30 a.m. The demands on the kitchen staff in preparatory work from before 8.30 until 10.30 are very severe. During that time the chef is particularly grateful for any extra help he can get.

The self-service store, too, has its especially busy time. Shelf-filling is particularly important and because Hussain is selling freshly killed chickens there is much light labouring work to be done as well as plucking the birds.

Hussain is a generous, jolly, kind-hearted man and the local young people aged between 12 and 16 have become extremely fond of him; to some he is very much a father figure. He remembers his early struggles and is a great encourager of hard work and determined thrift. However, because he had little schooling himself, he does not grasp that his respect for academic prowess and his desire to see young people gain good qualifications are not always compatible with his willingness to employ them whenever they wish. Nor does he realize that to some people he will appear not as a benefactor to impoverished youth, which is how he sees himself, but as an exploiter.

As the business develops some of the young people, normally boys, for Hussain has rather conservative views about the need to protect girls, have started to ask him if he has any regular jobs they can do. Therefore, he has taken to paying some of the keener children to help in the restaurant kitchen after school, but not after 8.30 p.m., and has allowed some of the boys to help in the shop, filling shelves. There is, of course, some interest in the poultry part of the business and before long some 15-year-olds are helping here too.

Gradually a pattern develops. During school terms and holidays the newspaper delivery is done on weekdays between 6.30 and 8.00 a.m., and again between 4.30 and about 6.00 p.m., a total of three hours a day for those children doing both deliveries. On Saturdays the delivery period is from 6.30 until 8.00 a.m. and on Sundays it is 9.00 until about 10.30 a.m. The children are all between 13 and 16, except for one who is 12½.

In the restaurant and shop the children are employed for two or three hours on weekdays and Saturdays and for the same length of time in the restaurant on Sunday.

All has been going on very cheerfully and many children have, under Hussain's guidance, become ardent savers of money. There has been no delinquency and no complaints from parents. However, not all of his fellow traders regard Hussain benignly. One day, to his surprise and growing horror and distress, Hussain receives a visit from an official of the local education department, whose first request is to see the children's employment cards, a demand with which Hussain cannot comply.

Reference section

Hussain is about to suffer a considerable shock. Although very particular about cleanliness and careful to obtain the necessary permits in connection with his business, he has completely overlooked the regulations governing the employment of children. These are founded on the Children's and Young Persons' Acts 1933 to 1963 (as amended by the Education Acts 1944 to 1976 and the Children's Act 1972). Local authorities have individual byelaws based on these acts.

Typical byelaws of which Hussain has fallen foul are these:

- No children (persons not over compulsory school age) may work in a kitchen or a hotel, cook shop, fried food shop, eating house, refreshment room, ice cream saloon or any other commercial premises.
- No children may work in or about premises wholly or mainly used for the killing or subsequent processing of livestock.
- No child under 13 years of age may be employed.
- No child shall be employed on any school day for more than two hours made up of one hour between 7.00 and 8.00 a.m. and one hour between the end of school and 7.00 p.m., or two hours between the end of school and 7.00 p.m.

He may well be in breach of other rules in respect of excessive hours in the shop.

Finally, he has failed to notify the local authority that he is employing children and to carry out their procedures, of which having an employment card for each child is only one.

Hussain is in danger of heavy fines as a penalty for his failure to obey the rules of child employment. A detailed study of the local authority byelaws on this subject is essential for any employer of children.

31 The Beach House Café

A reluctant departure

Maureen owns a souvenir shop and café in a seaside resort. Normally she seeks additional staff during the summer season, but this year she decides that she needs another permanent member of staff immediately to cope with increased business caused by the arrival in the area of large numbers of workers employed at a new trading estate. Therefore, instead of waiting until the late spring or early summer, she notifies a vacancy to the Jobcentre in March.

Soon after, a young man in his late teens or early twenties arrives and asks for the job, which he had seen posted in the Centre. He speaks with a strange clipped accent, although his knowledge of English is very good. He says that he is from the Republic of South Africa and is attending a technical college in Cardiff. When asked why he is not at his college, he explains that his course is unusual in that he is now free for nine months and will restart after Christmas. Maureen explains that she is really looking for a permanent worker, but when he says that he is really more concerned to have a job than earn much, she offers him a wage rather less than she had intended and engages him. His name is Peter.

Peter gives his address as a nearby flat. He attends punctually and works well and Maureen is pleased with him. At Christmas she expects Peter to leave, but he says that he is now engaged in writing a dissertation in his own time and might as well continue to work.

Early in February a plainclothes police officer arrives at Maureen's café and after speaking to Peter, escorts him off the premises. The officer briefly explains to Maureen that there is an irregularity in Peter's papers and that he should not be working. Maureen is surprised, inconvenienced and rather distressed, as she has become quite fond of Peter and can see he is rather worried.

Peter does not arrive for work the next day and Maureen,

remembering the name of the police officer, phones her local station. She is transferred to the immigration office and speaks to the officer concerned. He says he is on his way out and will call to see her.

When he arrives, he tells her as kindly as possible that she will not be able to continue to employ Peter, who may be deported. 'But why?' asks Maureen.

The officer explains. Peter came to the United Kingdom as a full-time student of a specialized branch of electrical engineering and his right to remain in the country was clearly related to his attendance as a full-time student. By the time he applied to her for work he had ceased to attend the college, despite the efforts of the tutorial staff and the college's student counsellor to get him to restart. The college was not the one named by Peter, but one in Bristol. His story about the break in the course was a lie.

By September the college had lost touch with Peter, who made no application for readmission in the academic year then starting. The immigration office in Bristol, carrying out an examination and updating of their records, discovered that Peter was no longer a student. Further inquiries had made unusually rapid progress and traced him to Maureen's café.

As he is leaving the officer remarks to Maureen, 'In a way, you know, you're partially to blame for what is happening. If you'd followed the regulations, then his failure to do the same wouldn't have gone so far. As it is, the magistrates will probably send him home.'

Maureen is very upset. But she has to be practical and she goes to the Jobcentre to give another notice of vacancy. As a result of her visit she is ready to cope with anyone from overseas who applies.

Reference section

On her visit to the Jobcentre Maureen obtained a copy of *Employment of Overseas Workers in the United Kingdom*. This pamphlet should be read by all who may consider employing someone from overseas.

If people from overseas, other than those from the EEC, who have permission to reside in the United Kingdom in order to follow a specific course of studies seek work instead, they are probably acting illegally. These cases are not uncommon.

Overseas students who wish to work during their vacations must obtain a permit from the Department of Employment through the local Professional and Executive Recruitment Office, Jobcentre or employment office. Their college must agree that work in the vacation or spare time will not interfere with their studies and there must be a specific post on offer for which no suitable resident labour is available.

Peter could not carry out the proper procedure because he had abandoned his studies. Had Maureen proceeded correctly when Peter applied for the job, she might have been able to save them both distress.

Appendices

I Equal Opportunities Commission

Head Office
Overseas House, Quay Street, Manchester M3 3HN. Tel: 061 833 9244
Scotland
249 West George Street, Glasgow G2 4QE. Tel: 041 226 4591
Wales
Caerwys House, Windsor Place, Cardiff CF1 1LB. Tel: 0222 43552

II Commission for Racial Equality

Head Office
Elliot House, 10-12 Allington Street, London SW1E 5EH. Tel: 01 828 7022
Midlands
Alpha Tower, Suffolk Street, Birmingham B1 1TZ. Tel: 021 632 4544
Manchester
Maybrook House (5th Floor), 40 Blackfriars Street, Manchester M3 2EG. Tel: 061 831 7782/8
Leicester
Haymarket House (4th Floor), Haymarket Shopping Centre, Leicester, LE1 3JG. Tel: 0533 517852
Leeds
Yorkshire Bank Chambers (1st Floor), Infirmary Street, Leeds LS1 2JT. Tel: 0532 434413/4

III Advisory, Conciliation and Arbitration Service

Addresses and telephone numbers of the regional offices of this service:

Northern Region
Westgate House, Westgate Road, Newcastle upon Tyne, NE1 1TJ. Tel: 0632 612191

Yorkshire and Humberside Region
Commerce House, St Alban's Place, Leeds LS2 8HH. Tel: 0532 431371

South-East Region
Clifton House, 83 Euston Road, London NW1 2RB. Tel: 01 388 5100

South-West Region
16 Park Place, Clifton, Bristol BS8 1JP. Tel: 0272 211921

London Region
Clifton House, 83 Euston Road, London NW1 2RB. Tel: 01 388 5100

Midlands Region
Alpha Tower, Suffolk Street, Queensway, Birmingham B1 1TZ. Tel: 021 643 9911

Nottingham Sub-Office, 66 Houndsgate, Nottingham NG1 6BA. Tel: 0602 415450

North-West Region
Boulton House, 17 Chorlton Street, Manchester M1 3HY. 061 228 3222

Merseyside Sub-Office, 27 Leece Street, Liverpool L1 2TS. Tel: 051 708 6626

Scotland
Franborough House, 123 Bothwell Street, Glasgow G2 7JR. Tel: 041 204 2677

Wales
Phase 1, Ty Glas Road, Llanishen, Cardiff CF4 5PH. Tel: 0222 762636

IV Department of Employment's regional offices

Northern Regional Office
Wellbar House, Gallowgate, Newcastle-upon-Tyne NE1 4TP. Tel: 0632 327575
Midlands Regional Office
2 Duchess Place, Hagley Road, Birmingham B16 8NS. Tel: 021 455 7111
Yorkshire and Humberside Regional Office
City House, New Station Street, Leeds LS1 4JH. Tel: 0532 438232
North-West Regional Office
Sunley Building, Piccadilly Plaza, Manchester M60 7JS. Tel: 061 832 9111
London Regional Office and South-East Regional Office
Hanway House, 27 Red Lion Square, London WC1R 4NH. Tel: 01 405 8454
Office for Scotland
Pentland House, 47 Robb's Loan, Edinburgh EH14 1UE. Tel: 031 443 8731
South-West Regional Office
The Pithay, Bristol BS1 2NQ. Tel: 0272 291071
Office for Wales
Companies House, Crown Way, Maindy, Cardiff CF4 3UW. Tel: 0222 388588

V Some useful booklets

All the booklets listed are free and may be obtained from the government departments concerned and usually from Jobcentres.

Any Act of Parliament mentioned can be obtained from HM Stationery Office or through a bookseller. These are not free.

Published by the Department of Employment
Employing Disabled People: Sources of Help
Employment Acts 1980 and 1882   PL 709
Employment Act 1988: A Guide to Its Industrial Relations and Trade Union Law Provisions   PL 854
Employment of Overseas Workers in the UK   OW 5
Fair and Unfair Dismissal   PL 714
Individual Rights of Employees   PL 716
Industrial Action and the Law   PL 753
The Law on Unfair Dismissal: A Guide for Small Firms   PL 715
Recoupment of Benefit from Industrial Tribunal Awards: A Guide for Employers   PL 720
Industrial Tribunals Procedure

Various aspects
1. Written Statement of Main Terms and Conditions of Employment   PL 700
2. Redundancy Consultation and Notification   PL 833
3. Employees' Rights on Insolvency of Employer   PL 718
4. Employment Rights for the Expectant Mother   PL 710
5. Suspension on Medical Grounds under Health and Safety Regulations   PL 705
6. Facing Redundancy: Time Off for Job Hunting or to Arrange Training   PL 703

Appendix V: Some useful booklets

7. *Union Membership Rights and the Closed Shop, Including the Union Labour Only Provisions of the Employment Act 1982* PL 754
8. *Itemized Pay Statements* PL 704
9. *Guarantee Payments* PL 724
10. *Employment Rights on the Transfer of an Undertaking* PL 699
11. *Rules Governing Continuous Employment and a Week's Pay* PL 711
12. *Time Off for Public Duties* PL 702
13. *Unfairly Dismissed* PL 712
14. *Rights of Notice and Reasons for Dismissal* PL 707
15. *Union Secret Ballots* PL 701
16. *Redundancy Payments* PL 808
17. *Limits on Payments* PL 827

Published by the Home Office

Commission for Racial Equality Code of Practice
Racial Discrimination: A Guide to the Race Relations Act 1976
Sex Discrimination: A Guide to the Sex Discrimination Act 1975